Successful Field Trips

Successful Field Trips

Mary D. Lankford

ABC-CLIO
Santa Barbara, California
Denver, Colorado
Oxford, England

Library of Congress Cataloging-in-Publication Data

Lankford, Mary D.
    Successful field trips / by Mary D. Lankford.
        p. cm.
    Includes bibliographical references (p.   ) and index.
        1. School excursions—United States.   2. Language experience approach in education—United States.   3. English language—Composition and exercises—Study and teaching (Elementary)—United States.   4. Thought and thinking—Study and teaching (Elementary)—United States.
        I. Title.
    LB1047.L36   1992   372.13'8—dc20   91-38558

ISBN 0-87436-638-0   (alk. paper)

99 98 97 96 95 94 93 92   10 9 8 7 6 5 4 3 2 1

ABC–CLIO, Inc.
130 Cremona Drive, P.O. Box 1911
Santa Barbara, California 93116-1911

This book is dedicated to all those teachers who understand that learning comes from all aspects of our environment and is not limited to a textbook or the confines of the classroom.

And especially to Chérie Clodfelter and Janice Summers, who are my friends and my mentors, and who are, for many fortunate students and colleagues, that highest compliment—teacher.

Contents

Acknowledgments

Teachers and researchers who provided information through their publications have been invaluable in this effort to link the field trip with writing experiences. Every attempt has been made to provide credit for all of these sources.

To those librarians who provided interlibrary loan service, I owe a special debt. A very special thank-you to Betsy Johnson of the Irving Independent School District Instructional Center for her diligent work in assisting with this project and for her interest, not only in the research, but in the successful search for resources. Jewel Parr at the Irving Public Library was Betsy's capable counterpart at that facility.

Responses to my questions about policies and guidelines in various school districts were provided by: JoAnn Bell, Richardson Independent School District, Richardson, Texas; Mary Ann Herndon, Spring Branch Independent School District, Houston, Texas; Winona Jones, Pinellas County Schools, Palm Harbor, Florida; Marian Karpisak, Salt Lake City School District, Salt Lake City, Utah; Anne Master, Norman Public Schools, Norman, Oklahoma; Pam Parman, Maryville Public Schools, Maryville, Tennessee; Judy Pitts, Fayetteville Public Schools, Fayetteville, Arkansas; Elizabeth Polk, Austin Independent School District, Austin, Texas; Sue Rose, Arlington Independent School District, Arlington, Texas; and Nancy Spaulding, Round Rock Independent School District, Round Rock, Texas.

A special thanks to my secretary, Karla Munroe, who has both the patience and perseverance to see this project to fruition.

Introduction

Why take field trips? A character in Charles Schulz's popular comic strip "Peanuts" once commented about a proposed field trip: "If you've seen one field, you've seen them all." The educational opportunities offered by field trips, however, are far more diverse than this somewhat cynical statement indicates. The ideas and questions generated by a field trip can provide a springboard, as well as the motivation, for active learning. The thrill of discovery is a natural offshoot of a field trip, provided the trip is undertaken with sufficient planning. Research for this book uncovered substantial evidence that field trips are an important factor in learning retention. Compared to passive activities such as television viewing, field trips are active and, with a little effort, can be motivational. By providing opportunities for seeing, hearing, smelling, and feeling—culminating with students writing about these adventures—field trips can complete the circle of learning. The ultimate product of such an educational experience will be students who understand the joy of questioning and who have a continuing thirst for knowledge. Most writing on education in recent years has placed strong emphasis on the following:

- The use of whole language techniques for teaching reading
- The necessity of students' acquisition of higher-order thinking skills
- The importance of writing as a communication skill
- Cooperative, rather than competitive, learning

Few writers, however, have dealt with the potential for using field trips to accomplish these goals. Despite considerable research on the rationale for field trips and the development of numerous site-specific resources, no single publication has provided unified information on the variety of educational destinations available and detailed methods for using writing activities in conjunction with field trips. The purpose of this volume, therefore, is to illustrate how to use field trips to teach and enhance writing and higher-order thinking skills, as well as to construct a framework of cooperative learning within which whole language skills and resource-based learning can be utilized. Teachers frequently argue against field trips, complaining that they do not have enough time to teach. This book will demonstrate how it is possible to justify taking students out of the classroom to spend a major portion of a school day visiting a museum, aquarium, factory, garden, fire station, zoo, post office, airport, historical site, theater, or library.

Using Field Trips To Develop Writing Skills

The skills of writing and reading are essential building blocks in all phases of personal and professional endeavor. Like reading, writing must be practiced to become a seemingly natural process. Noel Pazour, a former teacher in Boulder Valley Schools, Colorado, was quoted in the book *Creative Writing: A Handbook for Teaching Young People* (1985) as follows:

> I think children should write because it is the one activity which gives thought a concrete form which can be examined and improved upon. A second reason is that good writing requires a heightened examination of one's experience of life, searching memories and recalling sensory images and details, as well as emotions. This process can lead children to a more complete awareness and sensitivity to the things they experience.

Field trips provide students with opportunities to enhance their communication and writing skills. More specifically, students learn through

- Participating in the planning and decision-making process
- Engaging in writing activities that are built upon experiences
- Developing thinking skills through open-ended questions
- Describing these activities through writing

When students are involved in all phases of planning and executing a field trip, their understanding and retention of knowledge will increase. Writing activities are particularly important because they both clarify and solidify factual information.

Strategies for Planning Field Trips

As with classroom instruction, the effectiveness of any field trip depends on careful planning. The planning process consists of four steps:

1. Developing clearly stated objectives and identifying a focus for learner outcomes
2. Choosing a destination based on these objectives
3. Developing and implementing pre-trip classroom activities, including development of a checklist and schedule for the trip
4. Developing and implementing post-trip activities

In conjunction with these steps, it is important to establish procedures to ensure that students remain on task throughout the field trip and to develop extension and evaluation techniques for increasing learning retention. Researching and writing about a topic are indispensable techniques that serve this purpose. Students should be involved as much as possible at all stages of the planning process. In his article "Fine Tuning the Learning Experience: An Information Age Model for Excellence" (1989), David V. Harte, Director of the Learning Exchange in Portland, Oregon, alludes to the lack of decision making that involves students in the classroom. Such decision making begins with the use of open-ended questions—the type of questions that students must learn both to ask and to answer if they are to acquire higher-level thinking skills. Harte writes:

> The politics of education have given us too much "mindless and dissociated" class work requiring aversive controls. Too much class work is teacher-initiated, labor-intensive, abstraction-rich, and experience-lean. It has teachers giving directions that stifle inquiry-type dialog....Classroom deficiencies are reinforced on most field trips, because ineffective use is made of such outings. Participants at a

> 1982 science education conference agreed that museum
> visits are too often viewed by schools as an event, not as
> an educational experience.

Involving students in the planning and decision-making process allows
them to "own the experience," increases the learning effectiveness of the
trip, and helps develop higher-order thinking skills.

Organization of This Book

The first chapter discusses the purpose and value of field trips and the
various types of field trip policies developed by school districts around the
country. The remainder of the book outlines the steps for planning and
implementing a successful field trip: chapter 2 describes how to determine
objectives and focus; chapter 3 outlines choice of a destination; chapter 4
explains how to develop and implement pre-trip activities; and chapter 5
tells what should take place during the trip and post-trip activities. Also
included is an appendix with sample forms, lists, and other relevant
documents.

Successful Field Trips

1

Field Trip
Philosophies and Policies

As schools across the United States develop mission and goal statements, they are also defining the philosophies of their school districts. The development of a district philosophy is shaped by many factors, among them are economics, demographics, leadership, and student needs.

As teachers, librarians, parents, and administrators determine a district's mission, philosophy, and curriculum for the coming decades, they must keep in mind the many ways in which students acquire knowledge—visually, tactilely, and auditorily. The term *field trip* may seem old-fashioned in light of the information that technology makes available to many of today's students, but educators should not overlook the value of hands-on experience. "Distance learning"—learning via satellite, television, and telephone technology— enables educators to bring simulations of many sites into the classroom, yet these simulations cannot match the benefits of actually visiting a museum, park, or factory and experiencing its sights, sounds, smells, and textures. Thus, whenever possible, school districts should include a commitment to field trips as part of their educational philosophy.

The use of field trips to enhance classroom learning should be based on the following principles:

1. Field trips are a particularly effective means of gaining certain desired understandings

2. Field trips give students first-hand experiences that would not be possible in the classroom setting
3. Field trips are an integral part of the curriculum
4. Field trips should be planned as an extension of a classroom unit of study

Many articles on the topic of field trips revolve around the questions of whether or not field trips have value and what types are most effective. "The Field Trip: Frill or Essential?," by David Berliner and Ursula Casanova Pinero (1985), cites research by Australians Andrew Mackenzie and Richard White on the effects of field trips on retention of geography concepts by junior high students. The researchers found that active field trip participants learned and retained more knowledge. The article cites another study by U.S. researchers John Falk and John Balling, who recommended shorter, closer-to-home field trips for younger students, while citing novelty, unfamiliarity, and extensiveness as necessary qualities for trips by older students. "Both research studies clearly showed that well-designed field trips can lead to new learning, reinforce what has been learned in school and aid in retention of information."

Norris M. Haynes and others reported the benefits of structured field trip activities among a group of black preschoolers in "Benefits of Structured Field Trip Activities on Performance on the Peabody Picture Vocabulary Test (PPVT) among a Group of Black Preschoolers" (1983). They made this statement:

> Teachers should maximize the potential for learning during field trip experiences among their preschoolers by having prior and follow up field trip discussions and providing opportunities for activities which would lead to efficient processing of information, encoding and storage. A collateral benefit may also occur. If children, during their preschool years, are guided in developing an appreciation for the educational value of the diverse objects in their environment, they may develop more positive, sensitive and responsible attitudes toward themselves and their environments.

In "The Field Trip as Aesthetic Experience" (1980), Ernest W. Lee and Christine F. Myers urge teachers to avoid instructional methods based only on that "which is measurable, quantifiable, and empirically verifiable." Children tend to remember field trips because they provide opportunities to bring the abstract concepts presented in the classroom into reality. They are more likely to retain what they have learned through experiencing the sights, sounds, touch, smells, and tastes of a field trip.

Researchers Corey Muse, Leigh Chiarelott, and Leonard Davidman conclude their report *Teachers' Utilization of Field Trips: Prospects and Problems* (1982) by saying that

> the interpretation of the data offered here . . . implies that field trips can be an extremely valuable learning device if used judiciously. For certain learning styles, field trips may prove to be highly productive in terms of achievement, especially for students who are predominantly visual/tactile/kinesthetic learners. The key to effective utilization rests with the teacher's capability in organizing, sequencing, focusing and evaluating the field trip for the needs of each learner and in providing an experience consistent with the outcomes desired.

Muse et al. found that the school subjects most cited by elementary teachers for field trips were social studies (51.2 percent) and science (21.2 percent). The study, however, found no strong indication for field trips in any specific content area. Where cutbacks were indicated in the number of field trips taken by secondary teachers, "elementary teachers showed a greater preference for their present quantity, and balanced out between more and fewer field trips." The two most significant reasons teachers gave for not taking more field trips were cost and time.

Like other researchers in the field, the authors recommended pre- and post-trip activities and cited the need for developing clear objectives, utilizing the field trip as a unique opportunity for learning, and evaluating learner outcomes. They suggested that consideration be given to many diverse field trip sites. They concluded that field trips were important and beneficial if used judiciously. The key factor in the effectiveness of any field trip is the teacher's ability to organize, sequence, and evaluate the field trip activities to meet student needs.

Research has shown that many, if not most, students learn best through visual, tactile, and kinesthetic experiences; therefore, we must support curriculum and budgets that will allow students the opportunities to apply concepts and skills that have been presented in abstract form in the class-room. Field trips are an important means of providing such experiential learning opportunities.

Developing and Following
School District Field Trip Policies

A survey of school districts across the United States reveals that most districts:

1. Have guidelines or a district policy for field trips
2. Have a list of approved sites to visit
3. Provide teachers with outlines of a limited number of pre- and post-trip activities
4. Provide a student participation permission form
5. Have a suggested do/don't list

District policies range from a simple statement like that of Maryville, Tennessee—"All field trips must be approved by the Principal"—to lengthy documents detailing objectives, guidelines, and procedures. Some general principles apply to most districts. For example, since most field trips require school board approval or approval by designees of the board, teachers must make arrangements with their principals early enough so that this approval may be obtained prior to the scheduled field trip. Also, regardless of the district, only students whose parents have signed permission slips should be permitted to go on any field trip. The slip should indicate an acknow-ledgment by a parent of the nature of the trip and the time when the school's supervision of the students will end. Many districts have additional instruc-tions regarding what the consent form should include.

Safety, student involvement, creativity, suitability, organization, trans-portation, emergency procedures, and development of school board field trip policies are a few of the topics outlined by Theodore A. Chandler in "These Policy Tips Make the Most of Field Trips" (1985). He cites research by J. L. Mason of the University of Virginia that shows that

> field trips are an important link between the classroom and
> the outside world and an aid in learning. Because younger

students are less experienced with resources outside the classroom, elementary school teachers see field trips as a more integral part of their curriculum than do secondary school teachers, and as a result, they average almost twice as many field trips as secondary teachers do (6.59 trips per year, compared with 3.8 per year in high school, according to Mason's research).

Chandler advises school board members:

> Student field trips can be time-wasting junkets—or, they can be an essential part of teaching students things about the world they cannot learn as well inside the classroom. Your schools' approach to field trips, as spelled out by your board in policy and regulations, can make the difference. Teachers should decide the purposes and benefits of specific field trips, of course, but students should have some say about them, too. . . . The key to minimizing risk on field trips is providing adequate supervision. Legally and morally. "[A]dequate" supervision means whatever supervision necessary to avoid injury or harm that reasonably could have been foreseen and prevented.

The article outlines the following recommendations to assist school boards in formulating effective and equitable policies:

1. Because field trips can give students experiences that cannot be duplicated in the classroom and that can enrich their cultural lives, the board should encourage appropriate field trips that have educational value.
2. Proposals for field trips should specify how the trip will benefit students in a way not possible in the classroom, how the trip fits into the curriculum, and how the teacher will follow up on the trip afterwards. In other words, the proposal must specify the trip's educational value.
3. Every proposed field trip should be screened in advance by sending an appropriate teacher on the

trip without the students to determine its suitability and value.

4. No student should be denied access to a field trip simply because of the idiosyncratic considerations of one teacher or principal.

5. To provide equity for students and some degree of academic freedom for teachers, teachers at each grade level should prepare a list of appropriate field trips approved by the majority of teachers at that grade level. The list of approved field trips should be broken down into two groups: essential field trips and desirable ones. All students at that grade level will be expected to go on field trips from the essential list. Trips on the other list are optional, taken at the discretion of the teacher. Both lists should be reevaluated and changed as needed every few years. A committee composed of one representative from each grade level should assess the lists from all grade levels to avoid duplication.

6. The list of approved field trips should include all the necessary details for each: name, address, and telephone number of a contact person at the trip's destination; a map showing the location of the place students will visit; a list of potential hazards and safeguards; estimated costs; suggested ratio of chaperons to students; educational value to students at the designated grade level; and suggestions on how to integrate the trip with the curriculum, both before and afterwards.

7. School buses and drivers should be provided for trips within a reasonable distance of your schools. Any other costs should be the responsibility of the students.

8. Because it is not legally possible to obtain blanket permission for field trips, a permission slip must be signed by each student's parent or guardian before each trip. These forms should be provided by the

principal. The form should contain information that applies to all field trips; but it also should specify the potential hazards and safeguards of the specific field trip for which permission is requested.

Examples of District Field Trip Policies

- The Fayetteville, Arkansas, public schools field trip guide provides information on specific objectives, steps to follow, preparation of students for the trip, and follow-up activities, as well as a field trip approval request form.

- Schools in Pinellas County, Florida, have an approved Elementary and Secondary Field Trip List for school years 1989–1992. The list is annotated, providing address, phone number, and name of the public relations person at each field trip site. Administrators are advised that a request for local field trips not on the list should be submitted to the appropriate director of school operations and should have approval before any plans or preparations are made. Requests for out-of-state field trips require not only school board approval but also the approval of the principal, director of school operations, curriculum supervisor, and area superintendent. Eight weeks should be allowed for this approval.

- The Irving Independent School District in Irving, Texas, provides all building principals with a procedures outline for requesting field trips based on Board Policy EFD (Local). The list of approved field trips for elementary grades (1–5) is divided by grade level. That is, the approved destinations vary from grade to grade. All of the grades are allowed a maximum of two field trips per year, excluding a trip to the district planetarium. Walking field trips do not require central office approval.

- The Texas legislature stated in House Bill 246 that "instructional activities such as field trips are to be kept to a minimum and have specified instructional purposes." This statement is included in the Arlington (Texas) Independent School District Board Policy EFD (R) (Local), which also identifies the number of field trips allowed per grade level and general provisions. "No field trips shall be permitted in the secondary schools during the school day except for approved off-campus curricula activities not exceeding the class period. Field trips outside of the school day or on weekends may be approved. Except for vocational field trips, the cost of such trips shall be paid by the school."

- The Spring Branch Independent School District (a school district within the city of Houston, Texas) offers teachers an excellent 18-page brochure that states, "Study trips and extra-curricula trips are a very important part of the educational program, but due to the availability of funds, we are asking that trips not be taken unless they are carefully coordinated by the teacher and worked into the existing curriculum so that the most advantageous use can be made of our resources." Information is given on the educational philosophy that identifies trips that are "considered an integral part of the instructional program . . . ." (Art Center, Robert A. Viens Environmental Science Center, the Spring Branch Theatre of Visual Arts, and the Natatorium). "All symphony and opera presentations within the district are considered approved trips." Clearly written procedures for arranging trips, securing buses, and scheduling are included in this document, along with a cost formula for transportation and a mileage chart for various sites.

- The Norman, Oklahoma, Public Schools Board Policy briefly describes a field trip as follows: "A field trip is defined as any educationally justified activity where students are taken from the school premises for a learning activity that cannot be provided by any other means at the school. The Superintendent or his/her designee shall be responsible for developing regulations governing field trips." Among the general guidelines are the instructions that (1) all requests should be approved by the building principal, (2) transporting students in private cars is not allowed, (3) Oklahoma State School Athletic Association (OSSAA) approved activities are not considered field trips, (4) transportation is arranged by the school making the request, (5) overnight or weekend trips are discouraged and require approval of the superintendent or designee, and (6) no field trips will be approved during the last ten class days of school.

- The Richardson (Texas) Independent School District newly revised guidelines communicate to administrators the problems of budget constraints related to field trips. Although field trip funding has been reduced, these activities continue to receive curricular endorsement. Support materials for the planetarium, broken down by grade level, identify teaching objectives and vocabulary words and provide pre- and post-trip lessons, discussion poster samples, student worksheet keys and masters, and a test key and master. Enterprise City: An Experience in Economics, is a one-day field trip to a 6,000 sq. ft. classroom space in Canyon Creek Elementary School that provides students with "an opportunity to put into practice the skills and concepts that they have learned in the classroom. While at Enterprise City, students are the shop owners and bookkeepers for 15 small businesses such as a bank, newspaper, jewelry store, radio station, sports shop, and photo shop. The goal of each business is to sell enough merchandise in the shop to be able to repay the shop's loan from the bank." A checklist of things to do prior to the field trip is provided to classroom teachers. The centrally funded budget for Enterprise City includes the cost of transporting students to the site.

- The Austin, Texas, Independent School District Board Policy states that "teacher pre-planning must include teacher documentation of the essential elements (Texas state mandated curriculum) from one or more subjects named in the well-balanced curriculum. Teacher pre-planning must in- clude teacher documentation of the essential elements to be introduced, taught, reviewed or reinforced. Pre-planning should also include student preparation for the field trip." (See appendix A for an example of a teacher's checklist for planning a trip.) Other elements of the policy address parental consent forms and out-of-city or out-of-state trips. The policy also includes the approval request form. An Austin instructional memorandum expands on the Board Policy and provides ideas for extension of the learning:

    Some examples of extended activities include: large group discussion/questioning by the teachers; small group discussions with student leaders, leaders share with the whole class; the writing of an experience chart with students making contributions; individual drawings by students; a mural drawn or painted by students; journal writing, report writing or a newspaper article describing the trip; students formulating questions based on the trip (all levels of questions); a class book of drawings; letters written to parents describing experiences; dramatization/story-telling; and students should make use of the information gained and any new vocabulary.

• According to the Round Rock (Texas) Independent School District School Board Policy FMG (Local) "student travel shall be defined as off-campus or field trips and generally falls into three categories: 1. Field trips. 2. Extracurricular trips. 3. Recreational trips. School-connected student travel shall be categorized by groups requiring particular procedures to be followed for administrative approval."

• The Monterey Peninsula Unified School District in California, "encourages the practice of providing student field trips for the purposes of extending the instructional objectives of the classroom. In order to assure safe and stimulating field trip experiences, a series of activities shall be conducted to include obtaining permission from the proper authority, identifying safety procedures, setting instructional objectives, obtaining transportation, and providing follow-up experiences." The document goes on to establish procedures and policies guiding approval, staff time, and funding of trips, including overnight, out-of-state, and foreign country trips.

• Shaker Heights City School District, near Cleveland, Ohio, also broadens its field trip guidelines to include trips to countries other than the United States. "Field trips of significant educational value as a supplement to the instructional program shall be encouraged under the regulations established by the Superintendent of Schools. These trips may consist of any form of educational related travel within this and other foreign countries to extend the educational opportunities of students. The impact on the daily school program, cost to parent and student, student safety, and adequate supervision shall be primary considerations for approval of these trips." The regulations also state that the field trip should be directly related to the instructional program. The Shaker Heights District "Elementary Schools Field Trip Guide for 1991–1992" lists approved sites and indicates whether expenses are paid by the board, the budget, or the pupil.

- The School Board Policy for Bedford City School District in Bedford, Ohio, states in part that "teachers are encouraged to take their classes on field trips which facilitate the goals of the curriculum. It is suggested that these trips be scheduled throughout the year and planned for at the beginning of the year. Parental permission should be received for each student making the trip."

See appendix A for recommendations for developing school district field trip policies and for sample field trip forms.

2

Determining Your Objectives and Focus

Planning for a field trip must be based on clearly stated objectives and an identification of a clear focus for learner outcome. Berliner and Pinero (1985) describe this essential process as follows:

> Once you decide where in your curriculum a field trip would be useful, the next step is to develop a lesson plan just as you would for any other lesson. The objective must be clear: What are the students expected to learn? Without preparation and guidance, visiting a canyon can be an overwhelming and frustrating experience for 10 year-olds. There is so much to see, so much to grasp. The students must know why they are going and what they must observe while there. You can help focus their attention, tease their curiosities, and provide necessary background by showing photographs of the site, teaching appropriate vocabulary and leading preliminary classroom discussions. Plans for the field trip itself must *anchor* your students' experiences to the instructional objectives (emphasis added).

Without the connection between the field trip experience and instructional objectives, all other planning may be ineffective. Sherrie Brown

15

(1988) suggests that teachers prepare outlines or problem cards that identify specific skills to be presented. (See appendix A for a list of sample objectives and activities for a field trip to a dinosaur museum.)

When To Take a Field Trip

Do you take the field trip before or after studying the subject? F. William Sesow and Tom McGowan, the authors of "Take the Field Trip First" (1984), suggest that field trips should be taken in the first part of a study unit. They note, however, that many teachers schedule trips at the end of study units in order to reinforce the information that has been acquired. These teachers believe that waiting till the end of a unit allows difficult conceptual material to be introduced early while "students' enthusiasm and motivation are high; concrete experience is left for a time of fading interest; something to look forward to; the trip can be fully appreciated after reading, writing, discussing, and viewing." Sesow and McGowan feel that this approach contradicts theories of how children learn. They urge teachers to consider scheduling the trip at the beginning of a unit of study, citing Elliott Eisner and Seymour Papert's defense of the idea that

> children should be engaged by their teacher in a learning process that emphasizes their active involvement in a variety of "doing-trying-solving" experiences. Having direct, concrete experiences for students prior to engaging them in learning activities that emphasize abstract processes (activities such as reading, oral presentations, and informational writing) seems the most effective way to integrate these two educational "truisms" into a coherent instructional approach.

Involving Students in the Planning Process

Ask students how many of them have been on a vacation trip with their parents. Point out that their families do not get up one morning and suddenly decide to take a week off and go on vacation or move from one part of the country to another without developing a plan. Just as it is necessary to plan a vacation, it is necessary to plan a field trip. Emphasize the fact that planning is a part of any activity.

One method of planning is to divide students into groups and have them discuss how they would plan a vacation trip, building on their past vacation experiences. First ask students what locations they have visited on recent family trips and list these sites on an overhead transparency. Then assign one destination to each group of students. The categories may be broad (trips to the ocean, the mountains, a city, or a country) or more specific (trips to a theme park or a museum). Give each group of students a sheet of transparency film and a marker and have them write their destination at the top of the sheet and fill in their ideas. (Use water soluble markers so that students can add and delete items easily.)

On a separate transparency, write a list of questions for the students to consider in their planning and project these questions for groups to consult as they work. The objective for each group is to determine important factors involved, such as time, cost, and distance. Some questions to consider may include the following:

I. How much time can be spent on the trip?
    A. Are reservations needed? Who do you need to call?
        1. Transportation
        2. Hotel/motel

II. How much money can be spent for the trip? Money should be budgeted for the following:
    A. Transportation costs
        1. Fares for bus, plane, train
        2. Gas, if travel is by automobile
    B. Food
    C. Lodging
    D. Entrance fees
    E. Souvenirs, film, incidental expense
    F. Emergencies

III. What will be needed for the trip?
    A. Clothing
    B. Equipment such as skis, camping equipment, etc.
    C. Camera and/or camcorder, film, or videocassettes
    D. Passports or visas for foreign travel

Be sure to provide necessary resources such as maps, atlases, telephone books, and yellow pages for students to refer to as they complete their list of answers. Undoubtedly, they will come up with questions that cannot be answered with the resources in the classroom or the library. Discuss how they would locate this information.

After the groups are finished, project each transparency and have a classroom discussion on the plans for each type of trip. Ask students if any of the plans they have listed for vacation trips might also be used to plan a class field trip.

Developing Field Trip Objectives

A good starting place for determining objectives is to ask yourself what questions you want students to be able to answer after taking the field trip. Then ask students to identify the questions that they want to be able to answer after their visit. List these questions—both yours and the students'—on the chalkboard or on the overhead projector. As the list gets longer you may want to group the questions by category and divide these categories between class groups. This list of questions will be the basis for your field trip goals and objectives and will serve as a guide for continuing investigation of the site.

For example, if you are planning a trip to the zoo, your objectives might be to have students become aware of the reasons that we have zoos, who pays to support the zoo, and why the animals cannot be kept as pets. Students may want to know what kinds of food different animals eat or the locations where they may be found. For a trip to a museum, one objective may be to understand the purpose of museum collections and their importance in preserving history or culture. A trip to a historic building might raise questions about the architecture or materials used in the building's construction, e.g., many state capitol buildings are made with special granite and have such features as wood carvings over doorways or unique light fixtures. If you are visiting a cemetery, you may want students to understand what an epitaph is and perhaps to write one for a famous person from the state or nation.

In most cases, field trip objectives serve as a subset of objectives for one or more areas of current study. For instance, if an overall program goal for fifth graders in Texas is to become aware of their state's environment, a geology field trip could be part of a state unit in which students would

- Compare and contrast the regions of Texas

- Prepare a media report demonstrating knowledge that Texas was once under water
- Research solutions to the problem of water shortage in certain areas of Texas
- Identify sources of information about Texas geology and geography
- Record observations made on the field trip in a "learner log"

Understanding the Cost of Field Trips

If you are going on a field trip sponsored by the school, you can request that the principal come to the classroom with the approved budget and explain to students just how much money is available for the trip. This explanation need not be lengthy, but students should be aware that field trips require a budgeted amount of tax dollars—the school district must pay a qualified driver to use the bus and may also be expected to pay an entrance fee at the trip destination. Perhaps the budgeted money will only pay for the bus fare within a certain number of miles from the school. In order to help determine the feasibility of a trip, ask intermediate students to calculate the costs for the bus trip, based on distance, miles per gallon, and gasoline costs.

If students are considering a trip of considerable distance or an overnight trip, they should be aware that the school budget may not include enough money to pay all trip expenses. Planning such trips will require students to use higher-level thinking skills to make a recommendation about a trip's feasibility. One recommendation may be that the class must set a goal to visit a place within the state or to raise enough money to make a trip feasible. If the students decide on the latter, higher-level thinking skills can be used to determine ways to make up the difference between the amount covered by the budget funds and the actual cost of the field trip. Planning a trip, determining feasibility, and raising money provide an excellent opportunity for goal setting activities. Students would need to resolve several issues to obtain their goals:

1. How would students enlist a sponsor?
2. How would the trip be funded?
3. How would the class obtain school and parental support for the trip?
4. And the basic question for all trips—How will this trip benefit them educationally?

Keeping a Record of the Journey

You should discuss keeping journals as a record of the field trip as soon as initial plans for the trip are announced. They provide an exercise in writing, help students process newly acquired information, and allow students the opportunity to view their experience with different perspectives—during and in retrospect. In *The Young Writer's Handbook* (Tchudi 1984), Jessamyn West was quoted as saying:

> People who keep journals live life twice. Having written something down gives you the opportunity to go back to it over and over, to remember and relive the experience. Keeping a journal can also help you get perspective on your experiences. Sometimes writing something down, like talking about it, helps you understand it better.

Rules for Journals

Rules should be kept to a minimum because journals are places to capture one's own perceptions, emotions, experiences, thoughts, and ideas. Students, however, should know what your expectations are. Developing the rules with students is a good way to start.

- Determine the kind of book to be used (e.g., spiral notebook, blank-page book, index cards)
- Specify the format for each entry (date, author, time) (optional)
- Establish date(s) journals will be checked for content and thought
- Indicate the amount of writing required per entry (minimum number of words, lines, or pages)

Students must be able to confide in their journals without fear that they will be pressured to read their writing aloud or that the teacher will read and criticize every word. Discuss a privacy policy for journal writing in your classroom. Decide how students can mark pages that are private "for their eyes only." Emphasize that journals will not be graded on spelling or grammar. You may also tell them to put sticky notes on any pages that they want you to read carefully.

Blank books are the standard medium for journal writing. If students have access to a word processing program on a computer, however, they may prefer to keep their journals on disk, which would enable them to print only the pages they want to share with you—their other writing remains for their eyes only on the disk. Marilyn Cochran-Smith cited research pertaining to word processing in "Word Processing and Writing in Elementary Classrooms: A Critical Review of Related Literature" (1991). She reported "that using word processing, like using other software that invites interaction, has the potential to prompt teachers and students to construct jointly new social arrangements and new learning opportunities in their writing classrooms."

Students' choice of medium (blank-page books, spiral notebooks, or computer disks) for recording their thoughts is not important. What is important is that the description of the planning phase be included in their journals. Students should start by writing the goals or objectives for the field trip. The class may identify a general or broad goal; however, students should be encouraged to write their personal goals, or a particular question that they wish to answer in their journals. Along with the objectives of the field trip, any questions that arise throughout the entire experience should be recorded.

If each student has their objectives written in a journal, it will be easy to have students refer to their journals in order to maintain focus and to avoid distractions during the trip. One good technique for a journey journal is "dialogue journal writing," which is described by Barbara A. Bode in *The Reading Teacher* (1989). She cites one positive aspect of this type of writing in this way:

> Dialogue journal writing is a medium enabling teachers to integrate reading and writing in a whole language approach. It is this point that makes the dialogue journal writing so powerful for 1st graders as well as for other primary age children. It is one way to unlock the literacy puzzle. As children are allowed to spell with invented spelling, they are freed to communicate meaningfully at a more complex level (Read, 1986). As Sowers (1982, p.39) points out, "invented spelling gives young writers early power."

Dialogue journal writing, or conversing in writing about subjects of individual interest, encourages students to use language in a functional manner. Students can put their opinions in writing, pose questions, make comments, and use higher-level thinking skills without inhibitions. Bode suggests that students might like to begin this activity by drawing a picture.

Learning log is another term for paper and pencil recording. When asked "What did you learn today?" students frequently answer with the single word "Nothing." One way to encourage students to focus on their learning achievements is to have each student keep a learning log. This is slightly different from a journal—it does involve student writing, but it is more closely tied to student and class achievement because its entries must indicate that new knowledge is gained each day.

Marty Brewster offers several tips for helping students (and teachers) to avoid monotonous and trite learning logs in the article "Ten Ways To Revive Tired Learning Logs" (1988). "Students may want to alternate knowledge with opinion entries. One week factual information gleaned from the day's lesson would be cited, and the next week opinions about the day's lesson would be recorded." This will provide an excellent opportunity for reinforcing the skill of differentiating fact from opinion. You may also encourage the use of different colored ink for learning log entries, e.g., red for fact and blue for opinion.

A learning log entry about a proposed field trip might read:

> Our class is going on a field trip. I hope I don't forget to bring my sack lunch. The one animal I want to see at the zoo is the giraffe.

As the field trip progresses, new thoughts and new information are added each day. An entry may state a simple fact: "Tigers do not live in Africa." It may indicate the development of an opinion: "I wonder if the zoo is the best place to keep wild animals." It may address a question about procedure: "I do not believe we should worry about the money needed for a field trip." Regardless of its content, a learning log entry must illustrate newly acquired knowledge.

Using Open-Ended Questions

A Dictionary of Reading and Related Terms (Harris 1981) defines an open-ended question as "a type of question that is used to explore a person's understanding of what is read or heard, and that is intended to produce a free response rather than a directed one. 'What does the ending of this story suggest to you?' is an open-ended question."

The five "W's" that follow are essential in journalism and form the foundation for open-ended questioning. To these essential "W's" I have added an "H" for "how," a word that will allow students to move from potentially closed-ended questions involving "when" and "where" to more open-ended questions, such as "How did they move the elephant from Africa to the zoo in the United States?"

Who
What
When
Where
Why
How

These words are tied with the thinking skills that provide the threads for weaving the creative writing of students. If you are not in the habit of using open-ended questioning to stimulate thinking and writing in your classroom, you may want to use a "cheat sheet." Put the list of words on your desk or tape them in the gradebook so that they are accessible during class. Open-ended questions will push students beyond the literal recitation of facts and provide the impetus for improving their thinking and writing skills.

As directors of learning in the classroom, teachers need to provide a period of time for students to think about their verbal or written responses to questions. This "wait" time may be difficult for both teacher and students; however, the silence, or pause, should not be threatening. Students need the quiet time to think about how they want to respond before answering questions, verbally or on paper. So that this time does not become wasted "daydreaming" time, teachers need to urge students to use it to think and plan. This thinking and planning is also the groundwork for outlining and time management.

Thinking time for one student may be devoted to consulting the teacher or dictionary to develop a spelling list comprised of words that will be used in the writing activity. Another student may want to organize thoughts and clarify ideas by gathering additional facts from books, encyclopedias, or magazines. In both cases, the thinking-time activities allow the students to form their own knowledge base.

The emphasis on whole language as an approach to teaching has many teachers (and students) excited about learning. Jane M. Healy, in her book *Endangered Minds: Why Our Children Don't Think* (1990), offers this definition of the whole language approach:

> What is the magical formula? The essence of "whole language" is threefold. First, in accordance with current research in cognitive psychology, the learner is viewed as an active "constructor of knowledge," not merely a passive recipient of information. Second, reading, writing, speaking, and listening are taught as integrated rather than separate disciplines. Third, the materials used for reading, and thus as a basis for many writing activities, include fine children's literature and examples of good language in a variety of narrative and expository forms.

She continues with suggestions for improving students' ability to think by citing activities for metacognition, or thinking about thinking. "Strategies" is a key word in Healy's discussion of planning field trips and writing about those trips. She suggests the following plan:

1. Stop. Think. What is my task? (Identify the problem in words.)
2. What is my plan? (Talk through possible steps to a solution.)
3. How should I begin? (Analyze the first step.)
4. How am I doing? (Keep on task.)
5. Stop. Look back. How did I do? (Analyze the result.)

The following questions can be used with students as they write about the proposed field trip:

- What steps must we take to plan for the trip?
- If we made a list of things we must not forget, what would you put on the list? Why?
- How will it look?
- Describe your feelings as you plan the trip.
- You may have a brother or sister at home who has never been to visit this place. How can you describe the trip to them?
- How far is this place from the school? How can you find information about distance, location?

- Why does this place exist?
- Does it symbolize or commemorate something? If so, describe what and why.
- What are some of the things we may see on the way?

At the conclusion of these question-answering activities students have been involved in reading, researching, writing, computing, planning, setting goals, and working together as a group. Explain to students that they have followed all of the planning steps and are well on their way to a successful journey.

As the teacher, you have successfully guided and involved students in an important life process—setting a goal, determining objectives, making choices, and planning cooperatively within a group. These are skills that will provide a foundation for many other classroom activities, thus increasing learning potential. It may be easier to simply tell the class, "Next Thursday we are going on a field trip." Involving students in the planning process, however, will add to each student's knowledge and understanding of the trip and will build skills that are necessary to move through life.

3

Deciding Where To Go

Edward J. Zielinski (1987) stated that "the success of most field trips depends on leadership rather than location." Nevertheless, choosing a destination remains a critical part of the field trip process. Where are you going and why?

In planning any field trip, your first step should be to visit the school or public library. Enlist the support of the librarian or school media specialist in locating resources and information. Sources the librarian will have at hand may include

- Information on places to visit
- Addresses and telephone numbers (including toll-free numbers) for obtaining additional information
- Maps
- Art prints
- Books about various places

You may consult the Bibliography at the end of this book for many books and resources that will aid in choosing destinations and planning field trips.

Once you and the librarian have narrowed the list of possible field trips, you should involve students in group planning and decision making. Explain to the students that they are going to help decide which sites the class will visit. If limitations have been imposed by a list of approved field trip sites generated by the principal and/or the district, students should be given the option of discussing and choosing from the available sites.

Use an ice cream or candy store analogy to explain why the students must make a choice. They do not go to the store expecting to buy all of the candy on the shelf nor all of the flavors of ice cream. Ask students why they think the class is limited in the number of field trips it can take and list their answers on the chalkboard or on an overhead transparency. Their answers will probably include the factors of time and money. Discuss with them the problem of choices—we are always being given choices. How we spend our time and money and where we want to visit are just some of those choices.

In planning a particular type of field trip you may want to pose several site possibilities for class consideration. Divide students into groups to brainstorm ideas about a visit to each possible assigned site. Provide them with some guidance about factors they may want to discuss, such as time, distance, cost, and questions they would like to answer by making the trip. Assign (or have students choose) a reporter, an encourager, and a recorder for each group. The recorder is to take brief notes about the ideas presented. (Spelling is not important.) If the discussion centers around possible field trip sites, the notes would consist of those sites. If a vote is taken to rank the sites, the tally would be listed next to each site. The reporter uses his notes to report the results of his group's discussion to the entire class. The encourager's role is to see that every person in the group has the opportunity to take part in the discussion or submission of ideas. As an idea is presented, the encourager should compliment the idea and remind everyone that the basic rule in brainstorming is to accept all ideas. Each group must produce a final report that is signed by all of the group members.

Possible Destinations

The activities outlined in this book can be used with any list of district approved field trips. Teachers are encouraged, however, to consider sites other than those on the district list. Many such lists are not routinely revised, and your suggestions may result in the expansion of the list.

Sites Often Recommended by School Districts

Primary Grades

- Airport
- Children's museum
- City park
- Community services
- Dentist
- Doctor
- Environmental center
- Farm
- Fire station
- Goods and services—career education
  (supermarkets, bakeries, farmers' markets, sewage treatment plants,
  city services departments, etc.)
- Historic representation
  (re-creation of working farm, historic village, train depot, a home
  from a particular era, etc.)
- Hospital
- Museum
- Newspaper
- Post office
- Public library
- Restaurant
- Science and history learning centers
- Theater
- Zoo

Intermediate Grades

- Many of the sites listed for primary grades plus the following:
- Factory
- Law enforcement agency (FBI)
- Local resources (library, government offices)
- Mass media sources (radio/television stations)
- Military base

- Newspaper
- Police department
- Telephone company
- Transportation center
- Weather station
- Wholesale food warehouse/farmer's market

Finding Information on Field Trip Destinations

When attempting to incorporate exciting and inspiring field trips into the curriculum, you may want to refer to *Encyclopedia of Field Trips & Educational Destinations* (Long 1991). This resource provides a comprehensive listing, by state, of "educational links to traditional subjects, including science, history, geography, government, and the fine arts." A sample entry follows:

928 Museum of Fine Arts
465 Huntington Avenue
Boston, MA 02115
(617) 267-9300

An art museum with collections covering diverse media and historical periods. Features include nineteenth-century U.S. wartercolors, the Mason collection of ancient musical instruments, French impressionists, French and Flemish tapestries, American colonial silver, the McCann collection of Chinese porcelain, ancient Egyptian artifacts, Islamic art, European Old Masters, U.S. portraits, and ship models. Featured artists include Whittier, Cassatt, Goya, Monet, Eakings, Homer, Picasso, Velazquez, Warhol, and Renoir.

Facilities: Educational programs, gift shop, guided tours, handicapped accessible, lectures, special events, traveling exhibits

Schedule: Open daily except Monday; entrance fee, free days

Planning a field trip is a good way for students to learn about locating and using resources. Rather than doing all the research yourself, involve the class. All of the district approved sites can be investigated in the library, and, in addition to the library, your local Chamber of Commerce can provide brochures and information about many educational destinations. Publications by city departments frequently include facts about the city, its history, and contact persons for tours of city departments. These publications can sometimes be found in the library; however, if they are not available in the library, the individual departments can be found in the telephone directory, and copies can be requested. Federal agencies, which are listed separately in the telephone directory, should be contacted for their guidelines for group tours.

Be sure to discuss sources other than the library for finding out about places such as the local zoo, museums, or other potential destinations. These sources may include the telephone directory, city maps, state almanacs, Convention Bureau packets, and Chamber of Commerce brochures. All of these sources of information should be available for students to use as they research possible destinations.

Local Destinations

Organization Memberships

If you are not a member of the museum, zoo, or aquarium in your area, ask your principal to budget money for these memberships in the school library budget. Such memberships will place the school on the mailing list for exhibits and educational information. You may also consider serving as a volunteer in one of these institutions. In her article "Museum Adventures" (1991), Joanne Y. Cleaver suggests that if you "simply can't take your class to the museum, why not ask the museum to come to you? Many museums have staff who take activities and demonstrations to schools. These 'trunk shows' offer a hassle-free alternative to the traditional field trip."

Telephone Directories

Students may not consider the telephone directory a reference book; however, many telephone books provide valuable assistance for locating all types of information. The telephone directory is not only useful in providing information, it also provides a means for teaching students how to skim and how to use headings and subheadings effectively. Demonstrating to students that the telephone book is a basic source of information can be a first introduction to reference books. Many reference books, like the telephone book, have a dictionary arrangement, provide special features, and utilize headings and subheadings in such a way that rapid location of information is possible.

"The Blue Pages, Easy Reference to Government Offices and Helpful Numbers" is the title given to the blue-colored pages placed in the middle of the Dallas phone directory *The Everything Pages* (GTE Southwest Inc. 1991). The first heading within this section is "Helpful Numbers," which contains subheadings such as "Chamber of Commerce," "Consumer Protection," "Employment," and "Health Services." The next major heading is "Government Offices—City," which contains various city departments listed under "Dallas, City of." It also lists other suburban city listings and their respective departments. The last three headings in the Blue Pages are "Government Offices—County," "Government Offices—State," and "Government Offices—United States."

If your class were planning a trip to the Dallas zoo, students might look simply for a zoo heading under "Helpful Numbers" and find that it does not exist. A lesson in the organization of material listed in the telephone directory would lead students to logically determine that the park and recreation department, listed under the "Dallas" subheading of "Government Offices—City" would be able to provide the desired information.

Demonstrating to students how to use a telephone directory with its many headings and subheadings presented in specific formats, such as bold typeface or all capitals, is an excellent way to reinforce transfer of skills. That is, once students gain an understanding of *how* information is presented, whether in a phone book or a reference book, they can read and glean information more rapidly.

Many telephone Yellow Pages include such features as the "Finger Tip Facts" guide in the *Southwestern Bell December 1991–92 Yellow Pages for Greater Dallas* (Southwestern Bell Yellow Pages, Inc. 1991). This section begins with a table of contents indicating where information pertaining to emergencies, attractions, and entertainment can be found. You should encourage students to look at the contents page and point out how they save time by using the contents page to locate information. Under the "Attractions" heading there are many entries arranged in alphabetical order that contain information about the individual attractions, hours and seasons of operation, admission fees, and telephone numbers. Students could refer to this list for information on the Dallas Zoo, which is one of the entries. The size of the zoo, number of exhibits, and an "Infoline" telephone number are just some of the details provided. An area map lists the attractions in a numbered guide, so the zoo could be easily located, along with many other points of interest. The telephone directory for your city may not offer quite this much information; however, students should be encouraged to use the telephone book to obtain as much information as possible in planning the trip.

Before you assign students the task of making telephone calls, be certain that they have written out their telephone interview questions and that they have a place to write the answers. Students should introduce themselves, ask "With whom am I speaking?" and explain why they are calling. If the date for the trip is known, the student should ask if this date will be all right for the visit. Other questions may include (1) hours of operation, (2) cost of admission, (3) group rates, (4) whether it is necessary to apply for a group rate prior to the visit, and (5) times for special events (e.g., feeding the animals at the zoo). Have students conclude each telephone conversation with a request for brochures from the institution (one brochure for each student for writing activities) and be sure students are ready to provide the school address.

State Information

Most state governments have a department that provides information about places to visit in the state. State directories and state almanacs are available in the library and should list the address for this department in your state.

Matching Objectives and Destinations

Lawrence Katulka, after experiencing failure with the field trip process, decided, along with several colleagues, that a better system could be developed. In his article "The Boston Massacre" (1985), he identifies two types of learning that occur on field trips—"incidental learning and structured learning." Katulka feels that structured learning is the most important and that a field trip must fit three criteria to facilitate such learning:

1. The trip should be a close fit for the subject being discussed in class

2. The site visit should include primary sources discussed in class
3. It should be possible to develop questions that could serve as a walking tour for the site

By meeting these three requirements the teacher maintains the focus of instruction. The structure of the field trip follows the objectives established in the curriculum, and learning does not rely completely on the internal learning motivation of the individual students.

  Zielinski (1987) developed a checklist entitled "Should I Take This Trip?" which is an excellent way to begin planning a field trip. (A copy of this checklist is included in appendix A.)

  The remainder of this chapter is devoted to providing examples of trips a class may take to meet different learning objectives.

Field Trips for Art Appreciation

Art Museums

John C. Vitale offers ideas for art museum visits in "How To Keep Your Students from Yawning at Art Museums" (1977). He writes, "Of all the experiences to which an art student can be introduced to provide insights into humanistic expression, no experience has greater potential than visiting an art museum." The most important aspect of any visit to an art museum, he continues, is the planning that precedes the tour. He recommends that teachers planning an art museum visit

- Limit the portion of the museum students will see
- Point out different levels of comprehension that exist in paintings
- Move at a leisurely pace
- Do not start late in the day
- Avoid oversaturation

  Museums are always striving to make their collections accessible to young people. New York City's Museum of Modern Art has joined with Delacorte Press to produce a series of books "created to help very young people learn the basic vocabulary used by artists, a sort of ABC of art." The titles include *Colors, Lines, Shapes,* and *Stories* (The Museum of Modern

Art/Delacorte Press 1991). The books provide focus, and they can improve students' visual literacy. *Lines,* for example, points out that Vincent van Gogh's *Starry Night* is a painting made up of lines of color.

Zoological Parks

In the *School Arts* article "Art, Animals, and Learning" (1985), Frank J. Chetelat writes about the importance of learning experiences in which animals are an integral part. He recommends a field trip to the zoo to draw or photograph the animals. The four major objectives for consideration in such a trip are

- Identifying art concepts to be learned
- Preparing students by showing them how artists have drawn and painted animals
- Identifying your expectations for drawing experiences for students during their visit
- Determining how you will expand the sketches and photographs into activities after the trip is concluded

Possible pre-trip activities include

- Viewing slides of animals
- Stressing concepts such as line, color, texture, and pattern
- Comparing the Caldecott Award books, which contain drawings or paintings of animals
- Researching a particular animal and its habitat prior to or after the trip

The artwork created by students following the trip may include mosaics, stitchery on felt, multi-crayon engravings, or photojournals. All of these activities should be built on details pointed out at the zoo. In addition to artwork, written reports can be based on details noted while at the zoo or on those found in library books on related topics.

Artists' Studios

Learning experiences in art appreciation can also include a field trip to an artist's studio. In her article "Children Meet Artists" (1977), Elaine Levin describes a Los Angeles program that went beyond the art museum experience to show how artists worked. "The four groups of participants in this program—artists, children, parents and teacher—each found the experience rewarding, frequently for reasons they had not anticipated when the program was proposed." The author feels that future artwork of the children will reflect their participation in the program.

Field Trips for Learning about the Earth's Resources

A visit to both natural and man-made water supplies reinforces the value of life-sustaining water. Students are usually surprised to learn that they consume up to 150 gallons of water per day for bathing, drinking, and flushing the toilet. You may want to use the Water Tally Sheet in appendix A for increasing students' awareness of their own water usage. In "Water Works" (1988), Carol Van De Walle describes a two-part field trip in which her class followed water's route from its natural source into homes. Follow-up activities included preparing microscopic slides of water samples, viewing filmstrips on microscopic organisms, using books and charts to identify common organisms, and conducting water experiments.

The study of water also presents wonderful opportunities for students to explore the oceans, which cover 70 percent of the planet's surface. Whether you visit an aquarium, the seashore, or a community water plant, the knowledge students can gather about our dependence on all types of water will help them understand the interdependence of man and the environment. The subject of water provides a superb opportunity for an interdisciplinary study that can extend to art and music projects as well as to academic areas. Begin with books about the sea, both fiction and informational, which can be found in the library. Oregon State University publishes an excellent source—*Water, Water, Everywhere: A Guide to Marine Education in Oregon,* Second Revised Edition (available for $2.00 from Oregon State University Extension, Sea Grant Program, Hatfield Marine Science Center, Newport, Oregon; or as ERIC Document ED 275 539). Students can also write to their state or local water department, as well as other community organizations that deal with water, for information on water issues closer to home.

Field Trips to Geologic Sites

In "The Great American Geological Field Trip" (1988), John W. McClure recommends field trips using various state geological surveys and guides.

In most states, the guides, which contain detailed information, are "free, ... compact, easy to read, and up to date." The author describes a fantasy geological field trip that begins with stops in Texas and Alabama, extends across the United States to New Jersey, and then heads back west to San Francisco. (See appendix C for a list of phone numbers of state geological survey offices.)

Field Trips to Historic Sites

Katulka (1985) constructed a scavenger hunt field trip to the Boston Freedom Trail that was dubbed The Boston Massacre. Katulka's field trip emphasized the fact that pre-planning is "essential to creating a positive learning experience." He visited the site and constructed questions from personal observation that students were able to answer by asking a guide or by observing a signpost or informational marker. Students were warned that the answers might be found "in front, over your head, or under your feet." Learning effectiveness was increased by questions that tested the students' ability to reason. Both closed and open questions were included, offering students the opportunity to solve small puzzles and to use their reasoning skills. (It has been suggested that several sets of questions be created to discourage student copying.)

In an article entitled "A Field Trip to Gettysburg: A Model Experience" (1987), Mark S. Olcott uses a visit to Gettysburg as a model to expand upon the types of questions that should be posed to students, such as "How would Grant and Sherman, adhering to the concept of Total War, have done things differently at Gettysburg?" or "What effect might Stonewall Jackson have had at Gettysburg?" The author feels that the most successful trips are the ones that the teacher has taken the time to fit into the curriculum in a meaningful way, and he warns that a good field trip takes quite a bit of preparation. According to Olcott, the following list includes the most important elements of a field trip:

1. Preteaching
2. Identifying problems
3. Memorizing
4. Reteaching at site

5. Reading from a historian's account prior to and during the field trip
6. Using historical evidence (primary sources) to create a mood
7. Recognizing the efforts toward historical preservation
8. Solving problems and focusing on projects

In the Chester County (South Carolina) School District, fifth and sixth graders participated in a project called "Planning for the Future by Preserving the Past." The architectural walking field trips made students aware of carvings on the facades of the buildings and names etched in the sidewalks. Each child "adopted" a building and learned about it by sketching and photographing it, researching original sources, and interviewing people who could provide information about the building. The culminating activity was a field trip to Clemson University's School of Design, where architecture students hosted workshops that focused on the buildings the students had been studying. Writing activities allowed the buildings to "speak for themselves" on their past and future. For more details pertaining to this project, consult "Local History Project: Old Buildings, Young Eyes," by Susan Hopson Evans (1987).

Using primary sources to research historic sites can help students imagine what life was like during a given period in history. There are excellent sources of letters and diaries from the Civil War and other historic periods. David E. O'Connor (1983) states that "letters, memoirs, reports, and diaries are very effective—so are photographs and music. . . . I try to find old photographs whenever and wherever I take field trips. Photographs of the generals help students to keep names straight, for, at first every Civil War general looks like every other Civil War general."

Using these types of sources, students can see how journal entries can depict the time, the problems of the age, and the differences and similarities of people throughout history.

O'Connor also describes writing activities undertaken by students after a visit to the historic site of Old Sturbridge Village. The activities allowed students to move from abstract to concrete concepts in economics. Teachers identified "key economic concepts and understandings that could be incorporated into the study. . . . The students' tasks and responsibilities [revolved] around three timeless and universal economic questions: what to produce and in what quantity, how to produce and for whom to produce."

Field Trips to National Parks

Connie Anderson trained and toughened a group of five- to eight-year-old students for a descent into the Grand Canyon. They hiked down 3,500 feet—halfway to the bottom—for a round trip of 8.8 miles. Anderson feels that too much time is spent on paperwork and that unforgettable experiences such as the Grand Canyon trip help develop and strengthen relationships of young people. Her article "Adventure" (1978) describes how the group raised the money for their trip and the rewards for all their hard work. Anderson felt that Theodore Roosevelt's admonition to view the Grand Canyon as a national treasure and to "keep it for your children and your children's children" would provide the opportunity to set goals and to realize that sometimes goals include physical training and working closely with others. The trip provided the students with an "experience they'll never forget."

Students at some schools are fortunate enough to have a national or state park nearby. Jacalyn K. Wood, in the article "Take a Field Trip Close to Home" (1986), urges teachers not to allow budget reductions to cause restrictions on field trips; rather, she suggests planning a field trip to a nearby park by determining objectives and choosing specific locations as "learning stations," or points along a trail where students can identify various objects and make notes concerning their characteristics. Topics discussed may include rock study, tree identification, following directions, and observation. Prior to the trip, teachers should introduce students to the skills and information they will need for each station. Students can also utilize reference works and handbooks, talk to resource persons, and view films and filmstrips both before and after the trip.

Field Trips to Government Sites

F. William Sesow (1984) suggests the following activities for a study of state government:

1.   Begin unit with brainstorming session having students cite factual information they know

2. Hold planning sessions for trip to capitol
3. Focus on initial facts that need further exploration
4. Have field trip provide as complete view of government as possible
5. Incorporate small group/individual research on specific topics
6. Have students present reports/projects—topics should be generalizations formed by class or teacher from themes that recur
7. Shift instruction from specific to global, abstract questions and cover relationships between local/state and state/national governments

This model could be adapted to any type of field trip as well as to mock field trips, such as a "visit" to Washington D.C. or foreign capitals such as Mexico City.

Field Trips to Zoological Parks

"Looking Around at the Zoo" (1984), by James L. Milson, provides a worksheet for recording information and observations while visiting the zoo. (This Animal Observation Fact Sheet has been reproduced in appendix A.) The zoo, writes Milson, provides an excellent opportunity for students to learn "how physical characteristics, behavior, adaptation, habitat, diet, and locomotion all play important roles in animals' survival." He identifies open-ended questions to be asked and offers alternatives if a trip to the zoo is impossible.

The simulation game *Zoo: A Simulation of Caring for Animals in a Modern Zoo* is described in a 174-page book (available from Interact, Box 997, Lakeside, California 92040). The game offers students an opportunity to become involved in the daily activities of a small city zoo and to join in the battle to save the zoo. Activities include learning about zookeeper responsibilities, how to care for animals, design of modern barless cages, and realistic animal displays. Students will also learn about animal classification, endangered species, zoo careers, problem solving, observation, and interesting facts about animals. This simulation game could be used to replace a trip to the zoo, or as a part of a unit on zoos that culminates in a trip to the zoo.

Field Trips to Aquariums

Regent's Park, England, was the site of the first aquarium or public display of fish. Many cities now boast aquariums that display various sea creatures, and some are actively involved in research. In *Teach the Mind, Touch the Spirit: A Guide to Focused Field Trips* (Voris et al. 1986), the Department of Education, Field Museum of Natural History, suggests a theme for a trip to an aquarium may be "developed around the theme of adaptations to and the properties of water." It will take very little research by students to discover the amount of our earth that is covered by water. Through magazine articles and books they can easily see the problems of pollution in lakes and oceans. The objective for an aquarium field trip will be shaped by curriculum needs at particular grade levels. Objectives may be as simple as identification of various types of marine life or as complicated as the solutions to environmental marine pollution.

The Monterey Bay Aquarium Education Department has several handouts that provide guidelines for planning an aquarium visit. *Trash's Trek to the Sea* is an activity guide that encourages students to become aware of the amount of plastic our society uses and what happens when that trash finds its way to the ocean. *Suggestions for Chaperones* offers questions that encourage students to make observations, such as "What do you see?" "What's that animal doing?" and "Why do you think it acts like that?"

Pre-planning for a visit to the aquarium should include identification of species that are included in the aquarium. Once an introduction is done, students can then choose one type of sea life to research. Questions can be posed as to the endangered status, the changes in the environment that have reduced the number, behavioral habits, natural environment, and life span. Comparisons can be drawn between the cost and maintenance of a home aquarium and the cost and maintenance of an aquarium that will hold a shark or whale.

Combine literature with scientific study by using books such as Brian Wildsmith's *Fishes* (1968). This author introduces color and vocabulary as he describes "a hover of trout . . . a battery of barracudas . . . and a party of rainbow fish." The library will probably have more books about the shark than any other species. Encourage students to research other species using specialized reference books and encyclopedias to gain information. Be sure not to overlook the opportunity to introduce books about the sea and its effects on people. Armstrong Sperry's *Call It Courage* (1940) relates the story of Mafatu, a boy terrified of the ocean. It is a wonderful book for its description of Polynesian life and will provoke discussion on how to overcome fear.

If you are planning an aquarium trip, write to the Monterey Bay Aquarium, 886 Cannery Row, Monterey, California 93940 for an order form for education materials. These resources, priced at 25 or 50 cents, include titles such as "Recipe for a Successful Aquarium Visit" and "Chaperone Tips Sheet."

Field Trips in the Neighborhood

A field trip does not necessarily mean a bus trip some distance from the school. In "Hitting the Road" (1990), Teri L. Todd describes a neighborhood trip taken by classes at Lincoln Elementary School in Denver, Colorado. Bulletin boards and large-scale street maps of surrounding neighborhoods highlighted a schoolwide walking-tour program in which students served as tour guides and were responsible for pointing out historical sites, restaurants, and even their own homes. This program was designed to break down barriers, in a transitory school population, between parents and the school. Such interest in community has resulted in a sense of pride in the neighborhood and has helped to develop a camaraderie between home and school. Critical aspects of the program include advanced planning and publicity. Prior to the first walk, all parents received a notice that described the program, outlined times and dates, and encouraged parents to be at home to welcome the students during the tour. Newspaper and television coverage further increased enthusiasm in the project.

In her article "What? A Field Trip on the Playground?" (1983), Barb Garbutt identifies exploration trips that can be made without leaving the school grounds. She cites such activities as soil studies; sensory explorations (clouds, leaves, birds); exploring the playground on your stomach; a study of weeds; identification of insects, ants, and other things that crawl; and measurement exercises.

An excellent sourcebook for neighborhood field trips is *Open the Door Let's Explore: Neighborhood Field Trips for Young Children* by Rhoda Redleaf (1983). This paperback book is "designed to open the door to learning, not only for children, but for parents and teachers as well." Redleaf suggests going on walks after a rainstorm or on a windy day and walks that explore the community. She also offers tips for safer trips and sample permission forms.

Field Trips without Leaving the Classroom

Budget reduction, time, and distance are barriers that face all teachers. Sherrie Brown offers ideas for arm-chair travel in her article "Cruisin' Cairo!"(1988). She describes "Travel Writer's Approach (T.W.A.) as a motivational technique that encourages students to imagine that they are taking a trip to the country or culture being studied." She follows these steps in leading students on this imaginary journey:

1. Issue invitation from International Traveler's Club
2. Award $2,000 advance for expenses
3. Write a book about travel and receive additional $5000
4. Complete passport application (cost $50)
5. Fill resealable bags with travel supplies, including file folders (book covers), passport application, typing paper, photos, and self stick labels with "grant/name of country/date of entry"
6. Outline specific activities that are required and those that may be completed for extra credit
7. Prepare outlines, worksheets, problem cards, questions, and games
8. Prepare a bulletin board with travel brochures, photos, and travel periodicals and save space to display student artwork

Suggested activities during the "journey" include mapping, outlining, drawing a timeline, notetaking, listening, making math graphs, calculating distance, figuring out time zones, determining population growth, keeping expense records, identifying artwork (landmarks, special symbols, country's alphabet) and foreign words, and keeping journals.

After their "return," students prepare a book about their trip, with a title page, table of contents, glossary, index, and bibliography. Brown's article also includes forms for passports, health records, and expense records. (A checklist for an imaginary journey to a foreign country is included in appendix A.)

4

Pre-Trip Activities

Planning for instruction during a field trip is perhaps even more important than planning for instruction in the classroom. As the teacher, you will act as encourager, guide, and resource; and you will provide activities that will hone your students' observation skills. As you begin the planning process, ask yourself these two questions:

1. What expectations will I have for students as a result of this field trip?
2. What preparation must be done for or by students prior to this field trip?

Making a Site Visit

Just as you are familiar with the textbooks you use in class, you should be familiar with a field trip site. The site may be just outside the classroom or on the other side of the city; in either case, you need to acquire an in-depth knowledge of the site and its potential for instruction. Confer with the school and/or public librarian about library resources related to the destination, including fiction books about the site and/or any related topics. Informational books may provide facts, but poetry, mythology, and fiction not only expand interest and enjoyment of the subject, they also provide the framework for memories.

It is essential that you visit the site prior to the field trip in order to determine useful information such as the following:

- Time needed to get from the school to the site (It is a good idea to have alternate routes in the event of road construction.)
- Time needed to move from the parking lot to the entrance door
- Location of restrooms
- Location of eating facilities
- Availability of educational brochures that can be used in teaching
- Special exhibits available during the time of the visit

Creating Graffiti Boards and Webs of Knowledge

The framework for pre-trip activities can be developed with student assistance through graffiti boards or webbing, using the trip site as the key word, which is placed in the center of the bulletin board. The graffiti board is simply a place where students can write questions about a topic. It can also be used to write the answers to the questions once the answers are learned. Another approach to the graffiti board entails having students write what they "believe" they know about a particular topic and altering these beliefs once the true facts are learned.

The basic idea of webbing is to show connections within a network of ideas. A web is built around a central theme or subject, a single idea, or a book. "Webbing," "clustering," "schematic mapping," and "schematic design" are terms used interchangeably to describe a method of organizing ideas and elaborating on a central topic. It allows students to move from an abstract subject to a concrete idea that relates to the abstract. When creating a web of ideas, adhere to the following guidelines:

1. Clearly identify the main idea or topic. Print this word or sentence in all capital letters. Draw a square or rectangle around this idea.
2. Begin to brainstorm what you want the class to find out about the central idea. The more important ideas will be connected by a line to the main idea.

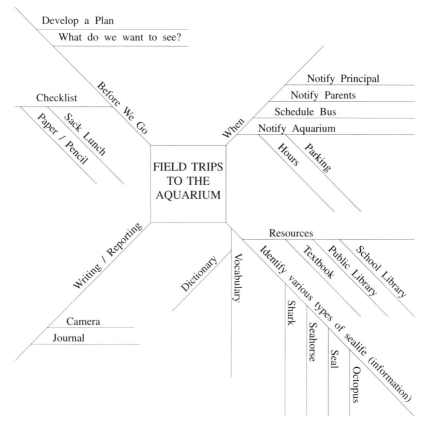

A Web of Knowledge Using the Field Trip Site as the Central Topic

3. Do not think about where lines or words should be placed. As they are generated, place them on the chalkboard or transparency. You can always combine or move them later.
4. Identify connections by using symbols (asterisks, underlining, etc.). If you use a square or rectangle for the central idea, you may consider using triangles for the next most important ideas.
5. Broad terms (e.g., introduction, description, habits, life history, methods of evaluation, etc.) may be written on a line connected to the central idea. From each of these lines additional lines with related subtopic words can be drawn.

You may want to have a handout showing a sample web diagram ready for this activity.

Identifying Questions

Initiate a brainstorming session to identify questions to be answered by the field trip. Provide a list of "starter" words to ensure open-ended questions:

- Define
- Compare
- Analyze
- Predict
- Evaluate
- Speculate

Creating Interest

Ideas and questions provide the springboard, the motivation, for active learning. The thrill of discovery should be shared by the teacher. No one (student or teacher) is expected to know all of the answers. Allowing students to see that you are learning right along with them will heighten student interest. The student who understands the joy of questioning, who has a continuing quest for knowledge, should be the ultimate product of our educational process. Create interest in a subject through

- Bulletin boards
- Audiovisual presentations
- Postcards
- Brochures from the site
- Posters, flat pictures
- Books, simulation games
- Writing activities that include development of questions that can be answered by a field trip

Other activities include

- Identifying vocabulary words students will need to read and write about the trip
- Locating, with the assistance of school and public librarians, available print and nonprint resources related to the site

Some activities may be based on your specific destination, such as the examples listed below.

A Trip to the Zoo

Show slides and/or pictures of animals. These need not be limited to photographs, but may include reproductions of paintings of animals, post-cards, and book illustrations. Discuss the different ways artists depict animals. Some of them create "true-to-life" renditions; some give animals human-like qualities; others draw humorous caricatures. Have students draw pictures of their favorite animals using each of these approaches.

A fun pre-trip project for primary students is to build a classroom zoo collection. Ask students to bring stuffed animals from home for zoo animals, and tell them that they should be prepared to answer questions about the "care and feeding" of their animals, such as

- Where did your animal come from?
- How much did it cost?
- What does it eat?
- Does it ever require a bath?
- Does it have a special place to live?

Encourage students to research this information in the library (make sure the librarian is prepared for the questions about animals and their habitats). Ask the students for suggestions on how to group the animals. One way is by type of animal. Others may include color or pattern of coat, size, and whether the animal is tame or wild. Have students vote on their favorite animal.

Ask students to develop a data sheet used for animal observation (similar to the Animal Observation Fact Sheet in appendix A.). Use the data sheet for research prior to, during, and after the field trip. You may want to offer students additional points for expanding on the questions asked on the sheet. In addition to habitat, food requirements, and care needs, other topics students can research include methods used to capture animals for zoos and descriptions of the animals' natural environments. Although districts usu-ally list the zoo among the approved trips for students in the primary grades, upper grades can also benefit from a zoo trip if it is tied to the study of ecology or endangered species. Older students can research the effects of disappearing habitats and poaching, or appropriating animals illegally.

A number of books explore what might happen if a zoo animal came to live in a home. *The Day Jimmy's Boa Ate the Wash* (1980), written by Trinka Hakes Noble and illustrated by Steven Kellogg, is a hilarious description of what happens when a student takes his pet boa constrictor on a bus trip. Have students choose a zoo animal and write a story about the problems they might encounter if that animal lived in their house. Then have them compose a classified newspaper advertisement to sell the animal. Bring newspapers to the classroom and point out the cost of this kind of advertising, where every word counts. Making the ad succinct—short enough to be affordable while conveying all the problems with and all the endearing qualities of the animal—will challenge the students' writing skills and creativity. This exercise also will provide excellent practice in revising and editing.

Discuss the zoo admission fee and what happens to the money collected. Explain that some of it goes to feed animals, while some of it is used to cover other expenses. The students can use their math skills to calculate what it costs to feed an elephant, or other animal, for one year. Similar activities would include determining the cost of food on a daily basis, employee salaries, facility maintenance, and the medical treatment of sick animals. Tell the students that the zoo raises money in ways other than admission fees and have them discuss these alternative sources of revenue, such as memberships and adopt-an-animal programs.

Invite a local veterinarian to visit the class and talk about animal illnesses and health problems. Although few veterinarians include zoo animals as a part of their practice, many of the problems they encounter are similar.

A useful book to use when planning zoo trips is *Zoo Clues: Making the Most of Your Visit to the Zoo* (1991), in which Sheldon L. Gerstenfeld, D.V.M., provides excellent ideas for aiding students in "delighting in the reverence for all animal life." The book is divided by type of animal: reptiles, birds, mammals, and primates. Each section contains black-and-white drawings focused on parts of the animal and concludes with statistics about that type of animal. Ideas from this book include utilizing the book's many open-ended questions about animals' eyes, jaws, skin, tail, and even nostrils. The author provides an extensive compilation of statistics, which lists foods that would be necessary if you invited, as an example, an elephant to dinner. This statistical information can be turned into a problem-solving activity by asking students to locate a source for, acquire, pay for, and transport food in such large quantities. "Veterinarians' behind the Scenes Info" is given for many animals. Students may want to invite a doctor of veterinarian medicine to visit the classroom and answer questions prepared by the students prior to his visit. If a visit from a veterinarian from the zoo is not possible, students may write letters or schedule phone conversations with someone on the zoo staff. Gerstenfeld's book is an excellent source for these types of ideas; however, students also may use almanacs, encyclopedias, and other books about animals to gather additional statistics and facts before embarking on a field trip to the zoo. Harriet Webster's *Going Places: The Young Traveler's Guide and Activity Book* (1991) is one of many books that can be used for this purpose. (A list of other titles on zoos can be found in appendix D.) You might also wish to obtain copies of publications sent out to zoo members and copies of *Zoobooks* (Stoll 1990), a monthly publication, designed to entertain and inform young audiences with facts about the world's wildlife.

More pre–zoo field trip activities include

- Locating nonsense poems about animals
- Interviewing someone who works at the zoo
- Inviting a zoo employee or volunteer to visit the class
- Writing to agencies working to save endangered species
- Visiting a pet shop that sells animals that can also be found in the zoo
- Researching efforts of scientists to communicate with animals
- Reading folktales that include animals
- Creating a graph to show endangered species and the numbers of animals remaining
- Using a map to indicate the native countries of animals at the zoo
- Organizing a fund-raising campaign to help fund the zoo

A Trip to the Art Museum

Prior to the field trip have students research the topic of art and begin their journey journals by making a dictionary of art terms, including different artistic media—watercolor, tempera, acrylic, charcoal, pastel, chalk, crayon, oil, and pencil—and the tools required by the trade—brush, easel, palette, palette knife, clay, marble, wire, loom, camera, and chisel. Also included should be terms like color (primary and secondary), value, line, form, space, texture, and perspective, and types of artforms other than drawing and painting, such as collage, mosaic, photography, sculpture, and mobile. This list of terms can be expanded at any time before, during, or after the museum visit. While students are making the dictionary they should be encouraged to use books from the library to learn about how artists create, where they find their materials, and how art materials and techniques have changed over the years.

Relate what the students are doing in art class to the museum visit. If the visit will include looking at sculptures, coordinate with the art teacher so that students will have an opportunity to use clay in the classroom prior to the museum visit. Discuss how clay models are made into bronze sculptures, and compare these forms to sculptures made from wood or marble. Discuss the ways weather and pollution affect sculpture. With students, prepare a list of questions about sculpture to be used in interviewing a museum docent.

Incorporate a museum visit into the study of a culture or country. For example, if the class has been studying Mexico or the Aztec people, visit a museum to view an exhibit of Aztec and/or Mayan pottery, gold sculpture, and clothing. In many cultures, people incorporate elements of mythology and folklore into their art and crafts; therefore, a museum visit could follow from or lead to a unit on mythology, perhaps one comparing the similarities and differences among mythologies in different cultures.

In the classroom, display and discuss posters that depict works of art from the museum. If art prints are available from the library, bring them to the classroom and then to the museum so that students can compare the original with the print.

Discuss the lives and work of individual artists, using books on art and biographies of artists. Discuss the relationship of artists' lives to their work, the problems they encountered, and how successful and accepted they were during their respective lifetimes.

Study poems and stories that depict the events shown in famous paintings. Discuss the difference between verbal descriptions and visual portrayals of events, people, or situations.

Plan a visit to the museum shop so that students can purchase a postcard of the painting(s) they enjoyed the most to put in their journals. Make sure that they know ahead of time that they will need some money for purchasing cards. On your pre-trip site visit, determine which artists or works of art are represented in postcard format. As students view each piece, mention whether or not a postcard of it is available. Letting them know before they go shopping will save time and frustration when they are trying to determine which card to buy.

A Nature Trip

Compare illustrations in books or prints of leaves with actual leaves. Use reference information books about trees to determine which trees may be seen on a nature trip. Balance the factual information with poetry and a fiction story such as *Tree in the Trail* by H. C. Holling (1942). Based on a tree that seems to be growing from a rock, this story presents the historical events that occurred around the sapling and settlers moving west. The historical approach may give students a keener sense of the history behind trees and of the strength and aging processes of trees.

Encourage students to contemplate nature through song and art. Patty Zeitlin's *Spin, Spider, Spin: Songs for a Greater Appreciation of Nature* (1974) provides nature songs to build appreciation for harmless creatures such as earthworms, lizards, and spiders. Jim Arnosky's *Drawing from Nature* (1982) prompts children to carefully observe plants and animals for the purpose of drawing, and Henry Pluckrose, in his book *Pattern* (1988), encourages them to visualize patterns in nature.

A Trip to the Beach

Stimulating interest in the seashore can begin with a small bag of sand, a rock, or a single seashell. Pose questions such as "What does the rock have to do with the sand?" "Is sand formed from rocks?" and "Is sand the same on all beaches?" Use the globe to trace the shoreline of states and countries and make a list of states that have shorelines. Use a webbing activity and have students describe what may be found at the seashore. Many students will be able to draw from personal experience, and some will even have rock or shell collections, which they should be allowed to share with the class. Compare the different types of shells—they may be placed in various categories depending on size, color, shape, etc. Older students can identify the scientific names for the shells. Locate books that depict the sea, looking under different subjects, including explorers, biographies, folktales, and myths about the sea.

A Trip to a Historic Site

Have students construct a timeline of the period they are studying. Discuss the sources they must use to add population statistics, clothing, or weather information for a particular era, including books of fiction or biographies. The development of a timeline will enable students to move from the abstract study of history by linking "real" things and events in their own lives to historic dates. Use Joseph Nathan Kane's *Famous First Facts,* Fourth Edition (1982), to identify inventions that can be linked with events and discoveries. The index by years begins in A.D. 1007. Advise students to look to almanacs for information on historic weather events, scientific facts, population trends, and economic data. If the historic site the students are going to visit is relevant to their grandparents' lives, have them learn the dates that their grandparents and great grandparents lived. Place these names and dates on the timeline, and use Isaac Asimov's *Biographical Encyclopedia of Science and Technology: The Lives and Achievements of 1510 Great Scientists from Ancient Times to the Present Chronologically Arranged,* Second Edition (1982), for factual information to add to the timeline. If students have favorite authors, they may want to refer to *Twentieth-Century Children's Writers* (Kirkpatrick 1983) to find the birth and death dates of the authors and to place their lives and works in historic perspective. You may want to suggest beginning with Louisa May Alcott and Mark Twain.

Taking Mini–Field Trips

Many of the ideas described in this book involve extensive planning; however, spontaneity and the ability to immediately build upon student interest should prompt teachers to occasionally take students outside the classroom to examine trees, leaves, cloud formations, rocks, or soil. Often 20 or 30 minutes spent outside the classroom will solidify concepts presented through textbooks or other resources. Such brief experiences, while building upon student interest, can help develop the skills that will be needed when longer trips are planned.

Such mini-trips should give students an opportunity to involve all of their senses. As they leave the classroom, each group should have a means for recording impressions, ideas, questions, and observations—either paper and pencil or a tape recorder. Their observations through touch, smell, sight, and sound should be recorded for further discussion or research when the group returns to the classroom. A practical guide to school-ground field trips is *A Teacher's Guide: Ten-Minute Field Trips, Using the School Grounds for Environmental Studies* (1973), written by Helen Ross Russell and illustrated by Klaus Winckelmann.

Developing a Student Field Trip Checklist

Student involvement in activities prior to the field trip is advantageous because it will help them appreciate the value of the trip. Having students create a checklist and discuss the reasons for including each item fosters involvement and, in turn, provides them with a sense of ownership in the experience, a better understanding of the purpose of the list, and a more serious use of the list.

Formulating a checklist not only allows students to become involved but also enables them to realize the benefits of working cooperatively in groups and provides them with a continuing focus on the value of planning. Students searching for the information required by a checklist will discover that information can be obtained in many ways—they will become more aware of the multiple resources that are available to them. Have students develop a checklist for all field trips, even for a brief trip to the grounds surrounding the school, because it can form the basis for students' formulation of a more extensive checklist needed for a more distant field trip.

Reviewing the Checklist

As plans for the trip evolve, the checklist takes shape. In order to help prevent problems on the day of the trip, send the checklist home on the night before the trip and schedule a final review of the plans with administrators, chaperones, and students a day or two before the trip to discuss the field trip rules and go over the checklist.

Other items to consider when reviewing the checklist:

- Is it possible for students to leave the bus at the front entrance?
- Did you allow time for a bathroom stop before leaving the school and before the return trip?
- How much time will it take to get coats checked in the coat check area?
- Will name tags be prepared prior to or on the day of the trip?
- Are tags preprinted with the name of the school?
- What is the plan for students who are tardy on the day of the field trip?
- What are plans in the event of rain or heat, or if a child forgets his lunch and/or permission slip?

In addition to the checklist, a map may prove to be an invaluable tool in the success of your trip. You can mark the route, time, and construction delays when you make your orientation visit to the site prior to the field trip. Notations about parking information will be helpful to both the bus driver and chaperones. (See appendix A for sample checklists and field trip rules.)

Writing Letters prior to the Trip

Although letter writing is a natural outgrowth of a field trip to the post office, it can be used for any site. Developing an informative letter about the trip to parents is another preparation activity that can provide a learning experience for students prior to a field trip. (Appendix A includes a sample form letter.) If students do not identify letter writing as a normal part of the planning process, you should include it as one of the necessary steps. In addition to giving students the opportunity to practice their writing and communication skills, it will give them practical experience with the postal service. Instead of sending letters home with the students, use the mail. Ask each child to bring one postage stamp. The school can provide paper and envelopes. (If a permission slip is required, it could be sent along with the letter.)

In order for students to reap the full benefits from this activity it is important that they compose their own letters and include the following information:

- The purpose for the field trip
- The planned events for that day
- Suggestions of ways parents can extend the learning from the field trip (e.g., another similar trip or a visit to the public library prior to or following the trip)

As an alternative to letters, students may send postcards to their parents. Use 4" x 6" index cards, which are converted to postcards by drawing on one side and using the other side for the address and message. If they prefer, students can cut out magazine illustrations and paste them on the cards rather than drawing. A light spray with a can of hair spray will help protect the illustration.

The letters requesting permission to go on the trip also could be written by the students to the school principal and to the field trip site. Using the standard letter writing format, students must communicate six items:

1. What they are requesting
2. Where they are going
3. Who is making the request
4. Why they want to go (objectives)
5. When the trip is planned
6. What the cost will be

Keeping Journey Journals

As Aeschylus wrote in *Prometheus Bound*, memory is "the mother of all wisdom." Willa Cather wrote in *My Ántonia*, "Some memories are realities, and are better than anything that can ever happen to one again." Much of our knowledge of history is based on journals kept by people who played large and small parts in events of the past. Many people believe that they will be able to recreate a special occasion or event simply by taking photographs and viewing them later. Such visual aids do jog people's memories, but written words do far more to recreate the event: the names of the people in the photograph, comments on the weather, a phrase explaining the sadness or laughter portrayed in the snapshot. You can give few better gifts to students than the habit of writing about the events of their lives.

Journal writing combines reading, writing, and thinking—essential elements of research. Using a trip to the zoo as an example, students can research the animals they expect to see at the zoo. After reading about an animal, its habitat, and its history, they can react in their journals to what they have read. They can record comments about the usefulness of books used to add information to their journal; for example, what entries in the index of books used for research were most helpful to them. Noting whether the information was current will make students more aware of copyright dates. These journal entries, written prior to the trip, form the beginning of their "story."

As students read and pose questions about information that they did not understand, they are learning a skill that is essential in a good reader—"questioning the text." The time spent reading and researching the field trip should equal the time spent writing. Nancy F. Browning discusses journal writing in her article "Journal Writing: One Assignment Does More than Improve Reading, Writing, and Thinking" (1986).

> After everyone writes for 10 minutes, the teacher may read his or her entry, emphasizing that there is no right or wrong way to write in the journal. Stress that the journal must make sense only to its writer, since the intent is not to explain or summarize the selection.

Browning goes on to state that "the only way a student can receive a low grade is by not completing the assignment." Grades are not normally given for journal writing, the objective of which is learning to respond in writing to a situation. It is difficult to place a grade value on writing that is supposed to express students' innermost feelings, thoughts, and opinions. Instead, you can use a symbol such as a dash to indicate an adequate response, with the additions of a minus (-) or plus (+) sign for incomplete and exceptionally thoughtful writing, respectively.

An example of an incomplete entry is "We went to the zoo yesterday." This says what happened, but does not express anything about what the student experienced. An adequate entry would be "The trip to the zoo yesterday was wonderful. We saw all of the animals we had been studying. I felt sorry for the lions because they were in such a small cage. I want to read more about building a zoo and find out what it costs." Exceptionally thoughtful writing rates a plus. Such an entry would be similar to "Our class journeyed to the Dallas Zoo yesterday. I stood at the place where the monkeys live for a long time. I saw six monkeys that are exactly like Joe, Bill, Frank, Sally, Anne, and John. They were alike because Joe is always trying to attract attention . . . (continuing to give attributes of fellow students, relating them to animal actions, etc.)."

A few writing tips in the front of the journal can remind students of techniques that will make their writing more interesting. For example, they may copy this poem by Rudyard Kipling:

> I keep six honest serving men
> (They taught me all I knew)
> Their names are What and Why and When
> And How and Where and Who

Journey journals can have all the elements of a book, including illustrations, index, and table of contents. The illustrations can be made by using brochures from the site, which can be cut up and used to create collages, or by using magazine pictures that resemble the site. Cartoon "balloons" can be added to indicate comments. Creating tables of contents and indexes will help students understand the value of those parts of a book. In order to produce these journal "books" students will need the following recording materials: notebooks, tablets, blank-paper books, pencils, colored markers, crayons, clipboards, and magazines and brochures for illustrations.

Another way to initiate writing is with a well-prepared teacher questionnaire that offers students an opportunity to work independently or within the framework of a group. Time spent developing questions prior to the visit can only enhance learning during the visit. The following are questions that may be posed to students prior to a visit to an art museum:

1. If you have never visited the museum, describe how you believe it will look, viewing it from the outside and standing just inside the entryway. Describe the floor, ceiling, and windows. Is the building one story, old, new? If you have visited the museum in the past, use your memory to write a description.
2. This is an art museum. Write about why something is important enough to be housed in a museum. Will you want to see paintings, objects such as masks, bowls, and jewelry, or furnishings?

3. How do museums obtain their collections? This may be a research question. Use a library and work independently to write your answer.
4. Who built the very first museum? Why was it built? If you had the money to build a museum, what kind of collection would you place in it? How would you raise the money to continue to support the museum?
5. When we visit the museum, we will have an opportunity to view some paintings. You will choose one painting to describe (color, shape, objects, or people in the painting). Look at one book from the library that shows illustrations of famous paintings. Choose one painting and write about it.
6. In the museum you will see guards and tour guides. Be ready to describe their jobs. You should ask them some questions. Jot down one question that you will want to ask.
7. Each age and each country has produced art in a variety of forms. Choose a country and research its art and artists. When we visit the museum, ask if the collection includes any art from that country. Write about one object.

These types of questions provide choices for students and prevent them from looking for the "right" answer.

In the article "Cruisin' Cairo!" (1988), Sherrie Brown describes the writing activities of her class as they took an imaginary trip to Cairo. Students decorated the front of file folders that contained their passport application, complete with student photograph; an outline map of Egypt; an outline to assist students in framing their writing; math activity pages for recording expenses; story starters such as "A Funny Thing Happened on My Way to (place)," "Getting To Know (place) the Hard Way," and "What NOT To Do in (place)." The class made decisions about the sequence of information to be included in the file folder book, and, according to the article, each of the students also prepared a guide book that included all of the components of a real book—title page, table of contents, chapters, glossary, index, and bibliography. These guides were submitted at various stages of completion for evaluation by the teacher. They were checked for organization, extra effort, and how thoroughly the work had been done. The books were graded and students given a "check" or paper money for the work they did in writing them. The money was then used to "pay" the teacher to gain additional time for fun activities, such as reading, recess, or special art projects. Although Brown's class trip was imaginary, these same techniques will work with an actual trip.

Building Vocabulary

Lucy Calkins, cited by Kalli Desmarteau Dakos in her article "What's There To Write About?" (1987), says that teachers can "tap the human urge to write if we can help students realize their lives are worth writing about." Beginning with planning the trip, students can develop vocabulary lists to keep in their journal notebooks. You should tell them to include words of emotion and feeling (excitement, fright, joy), thereby reinforcing the importance of their individual thoughts, interests, and feelings. This mini-dictionary will serve as a resource for students as they record their impressions of the field trip. You may want students to turn their notebooks upside down so that their dictionary begins at the back of the journal and all of the paper in the notebook can be used (front and back). Have them designate a place halfway or two-thirds from the back of the book for the beginning of the dictionary. Creating a dictionary serves several purposes:

1. The teacher will not be repeatedly asked how to spell words
2. Spelling in the journals will improve
3. The importance of a dictionary will be reinforced
4. Vocabulary will improve as students assist each other in adding words to their dictionaries

Developing Observation Skills

World War II is not an appropriate subject for a term paper, or even a book, because the scope is too great. An individual attempting to write on this topic would have to concentrate on one particular aspect such as a person or an event. Similarly, students should learn how to narrow their topics and focus their observations before going on a field trip. Encourage students to take one item—a tree, a shrub, or a 36" x 36" block of land—and learn as much as they can about that one object or area. If a student is focusing on a tree, encourage her or him to begin by writing words that would describe the parts of the tree to someone who is unable to see it. How does the tree feel? How does it smell? Such observation exercises also encourage vocabulary development. Keep a pocket thesaurus or dictionary available for students who need assistance with a word or synonym. Explain to the class that this same technique can be used in a museum. Students who describe, in detail, one painting, or one exhibit at a natural history museum can also expand their writing to include how they feel about that exhibit. It is important to give students the opportunuty to practice on single objects to narrow their focus prior to the trip so that they realize they are not expected to write about all of the objects they see during the trip.

Students can also practice observation skills as they make the trip from home to school, then record their observations in their journals. What do they really see? They should aim to answer such questions as the following:

- How many mailboxes are there?
- Are the mailboxes on the north, south, east, or west side of the street?
- Why are the mailboxes placed where they are? Who decides on their placement?
- Are there shops, gasoline stations, parks, rivers, traffic lights, fire stations?
- Where should they go if they needed assistance on the walk from school to home?
- What are the names of all the streets they cross? How are streets named?
- Are there fast food restaurants on the way to school? Describe the food served and the smell of the food.

Making Audio and Video Recordings

If audio- or videotapes are to be used as a part of the field trip, students should be given the opportunity to become comfortable with the operation of the equipment. This instruction should be planned as part of the pre-trip experience. Along with becoming comfortable with the equipment, students should also be responsible for scheduling and making sure the equipment is available for their use on the date of the trip.

Audio- and especially videotaping are popular methods for recording events. This instant audio/video scrapbook should not be automatically eliminated because it is not the traditional pen-and-paper method of reporting, but you should explain to the class that it may not facilitate satisfactory reflection on feelings about the event. Following the field trip, have students write a script to support the video. This will allow them to expand on the visual portion of the tape—the script should not simply describe what is shown visually. Writing should be used to synthesize and evaluate a field trip because, in addition to improving writing skills, it helps students assimilate and process the experience.

Bernice E. Cullinan, in *Literature and the Child,* Second Edition (1989), describes the positive results of student-made books. She concludes her discussion of "blank" books with these statements: "Keeping a journal develops and extends writing skills" and "Individual or group diaries can record events, thoughts, ideas, and plans." Audio and video recording can serve as a visual memory for the event, but it is important to encourage students to reflect on the trip as a part of the writing experience.

Predicting Success

Prior to the trip you may want to discuss prediction with the students. If they are not certain what a prediction is, you may want to define it. Ask students to work in groups and make predictions based on the following questions:

1. How many students will be unable to go on the trip? (This may be due to illness, or other family emergencies.)
2. How many students will not remember to bring their permission slips?
3. How many students will forget to bring their sack lunch?
4. Will anyone get lost during the visit?
5. Will all of the questions listed on the chalkboard be answered?
6. What will the total cost for the trip be? Include bus transportation, entrance fees, and lunch.

As a culmination to this predictive activity you may want to make a checklist based on the students' predictions. Include items they must remember for the trip: permission slips, money, times of departure and return. Upon return from the field trip, the class can determine whether their predictions were accurate. The primary purpose of this checklist is to bring the predictive activity into an experience where the results can not only be checked, but where they are also relevant to the students.

5

Activities during
and after the Trip

Developing the Trip Schedule

A field trip is more successful and enjoyable for everyone if a basic time schedule is developed ahead of time. (A sample field trip schedule is included in appendix A.) It is particularly important that parents and students know the times of departure from and return to the school and that these times do not change, yet the schedule should allow for some flexibility. The students may find something particularly interesting and want to spend additional time viewing or reading about a display. Throughout the trip continue to monitor student interest and adjust the schedule accordingly. Be prepared to answer and ask questions to maintain student involvement. Listen, so that you can be certain students are not gaining misinformation from casual observation of the subject or from the comments of other students.

With younger students, build in frequent Q & A times throughout the schedule. Include blocks of time for students to draw or sketch pictures and/or write in their journals.

Notetaking, recording, and photography can be used with several different types of data sheets. (The Animal Observation Fact Sheet in appendix A is a good example of a data sheet for a trip to the zoo.) These data sheets, or checklists, should not be used exclusively but can serve as memory joggers. If students have been working in small groups prior to the trip, they should maintain that grouping while on the trip. In these groups students can work easily on group activities as well as on their own individual activities. For example, one member of each group can use the checklist while other group members can take notes. Small groups will also enable adult chaperones to be responsible for fewer students.

Processing, Linking, and Learning

Andrew A. MacKenzie's and Richard T. White's "Fieldwork in Geography and Long-Term Memory Structures" (1982) describes a study based on the model of memory proposed by Gagne and White.

> Gagne and White (1978) proposed that people's long-term memory stores should be considered to contain four types of element: verbal knowledge, intellectual skills, images, and episodes. Verbal knowledge consists of facts or beliefs, and may also be termed propositional knowledge. Intellectual skills are memories of how to perform a class of tasks, such as constructing a profile between two points from a contour map, in contrast to memory of a single fact. Images are visual or diagrammatic representations of information in memory, and episodes are memories of events in which the individual took part. Gagne and White postulate that recall of any element is a function of its degree of interlinking in memory with other elements, and, as a specific instance, that newly acquired verbal knowledge and intellectual skills will be retained better if they are associated with easily recalled episodes. Well-conducted field work should provide students with clear episodes, and thus the Gagne and White theory implies that field work should improve retention of related factual knowledge and skills.

Students can go on a field trip, however, and not form stable episodes, or they can fail to link any episode that they do form with other knowledge.

Wittrock (1974) argues that all effective learning involves the student in generating meaning for the new information or experience by relating it to prior knowledge; the student must be active in processing the new material. Few geography excursions are planned with this precept as the guiding principle, so there is an opportunity to develop new styles of excursion that do concentrate on processing, or generation of meaning.

The MacKenzie and White study tested several hypotheses. One of these was that

> with respect to performance on a test of retention of knowledge, fieldwork which encourages processing will be superior to fieldwork which does not, and both will be superior to instruction without fieldwork. . . . The important hypothesis in this investigation is hypothesis 3, concerning the effect of fieldwork processing on retention of related subject matter. This is confirmed, and the size of the effect is remarkable. . . . If the retention test means are expressed as a percentage of the initial achievement test mean, the processing group shows 90 percent retention, in marked contrast to the traditional group with 48 percent and the control group with 51 percent.
>
> From Andrew A. MacKenzie and Richard T. White. "Fieldwork in Geography and Long-Term Memory Structures." *American Educational Research Journal* 19 (Winter 1982): 623–632. Copyright © 1982 by the American Educational Research Association. Reprinted with permission of the publisher.

As you encourage students to write and draw about their experiences prior to and following the field trip, you are encouraging them to exercise their ability to build on prior learning, to link the experience to something concrete, and to reinforce that learning by writing or artistically recreating that experience to ensure retention of the knowledge.

Post-Trip Activities

Ideas for post-trip activities evolve as the planning for the field trip progresses. The following are just a few examples of the many possible activities that help to expand on the knowledge that students have gained during the field trip:

- Evaluating the field trip
- Expanding on ideas from student journals or learning logs
- Creating a photo essay of the trip
- Identifying unresolved questions that may be answered through additional research in the library
- Writing activities

Evaluating the Field Trip

Evaluation of any set of experiences provides

- An opportunity to assess understanding of the experience
- An opportunity to correct any misinformation
- An opportunity to place the knowledge gained in perspective (chronological, geographical, cultural)
- An opportunity to reteach
- An opportunity to avoid mistakes in planning this experience for other students

Student evaluation should take place immediately after the trip. Write their comments, words, observations, and problems on a transparency to encourage brainstorming.

Writing as a Response to the Field Trip

The Teacher's Journal

Keeping a teacher journal about the field trip experience provides an opportunity to model writing for students, serves as an aid in improving the next trip, and provides opportunities to advise other teachers of pitfalls. In an article in *Nature Study* (1984), Richard B. Fischer refers to the "field notebook," which can be utilized like the lesson plan book:

You know what you want the class to learn from the trip, therefore, you have been able to write questions in your field notebook that will elicit the answers which will constitute the subject matter of the trip. Instead of merely dispensing information, you make the learners examine. You make them describe. You make them compare. When you do that you force them to involve themselves in the learning. Involved learners are not only excited learners, but they are exciting to watch as they learn.

Getting Started with Writing Activities

The U.S. Department of Education, in *What Works: Research about Teaching and Learning* (1986), states that "the most effective way to teach writing is to teach it as a process of brainstorming, composing, revising, and editing" and that "students learn to write well through frequent practice." A well-structured assignment has a meaningful topic, a clear sense of purpose, and a real audience. "Good writing assignments are often an extension of class reading, discussion, and activities; not isolated exercises." An effective writing lesson contains these elements:

1. Brainstorming: Students think and talk about their topics. They collect information and ideas, often much more than they will finally use. They sort through their ideas to organize and clarify what they want to say.
2. Composing: Students compose a first draft. This part is typically time consuming and difficult, even for good writers.
3. Revising: Students re-read what they have written, sometimes collecting responses from teachers, classmates, parents, and others. The most useful teacher response to an early draft focuses on what students are trying to say, not the mechanics of writing. Teachers can help most by asking for clarification, commenting on vivid expressions or fresh ideas, and suggesting ways to support the main thrust of the writing. Students can then consider the feedback and decide how to use it to improve the next draft.
4. Editing: Students check their final version for spelling, grammar, punctuation, other writing mechanics, and legibility.

Prompt feedback from teachers on written assignments is important in building student interest in the writing process. Speedy completion of writing projects combined with positive reinforcement will demonstrate to students that writing does not have to be a long, drawn-out activity. Students are most likely to write competently when schools routinely require writing in all subject areas, not just in English class. Writing becomes a natural part of learning when all aspects of daily classroom activities are described with written words, phrases, sentences, and paragraphs. When you ask "What do we know now?" and write the answer on the chalkboard or overhead transparency, you are modeling the use of words to clarify meaning, an important means of communication, and a way to keep a record of progress. When you ask students for "a better word" in these activities, you place emphasis on words and their importance and reinforce skills in the use of the dictionary and thesaurus.

Martha Lockard cites the following chart for prewriting as she outlines Dr. Calvin Taylor's multiple talent writing process in "PencilTip Talents" (1990):

Talent	*Prewriting Technique*
Productive Thinking	Brainstorming, free-writing, wet ink writing, experimenting, listing, reader's response to literature, scribbling, dreaming
Communication	Listing, sentence stubs, dialogue, traveling tales, drama, art, impressions
Forecasting	Looping, what if . . . writing
Planning	Listing, rhetorical strategies
Decision Making	Topic search, note taking, research
	Talking, listening, and responding in a journal or learning log are important composing tools in all talent areas during prewriting.

Using this framework, students can reflect on their field trip experiences. As they complete their writing, editing, and rewriting, you should consider "publishing" the best works and placing them in the school library. This publishing venture should require the same stringent scrutiny that any published work receives. Adding the book to the library collection should be a cooperative project with the school librarian that includes all the necessary steps to process a book for circulation (book pocket, book card, call number, bar code).

As in the planning process, use open-ended questions to stimulate students to think and write about their experience. Encourage them to use a dictionary and/or a thesaurus to find the best words to use in their descriptions. Some examples of questions follow:

- Describe how the place looked.
- How did you feel when you arrived? How did you feel when you were on your way back to school?
- Describe why you would like to visit this place again.
- Write a letter from one of the inhabitants to you (this can be from an animal at the zoo).
- Describe a symbol you could make that would represent the place, such as a flag, logo, letterhead, doll, or mug.
- There were many souvenirs for sale at the place we visited. Did any of them represent the place? Why not?
- Describe the smells you remember that were representative of the place.
- Describe the noises heard at the place. What was the cause of the noises? How did these noises affect your feeling about the trip?
- You have decided to donate a large amount of money to the place we have just visited. How would you suggest that the money be spent? Why?

For a historic site:

- Would you like to have lived in that age? Why? Why not? What would have been different in your life if you had lived then?
- What technology do we have now that they did not have? How would that technology have changed their everyday lives?

For another exercise, give each student a picture postcard. Ask them to read the brief description of the picture on the postcard and then write a similar description of the place they have visited.

Webbing

Spinning a web can be done as a pre-trip activity or as a way to recall events after the trip. Before asking the class to write about their field trip experience, conduct a webbing activity. It will give students a chance to organize their thoughts or topics and to extend thinking. It can also assist students in moving from the abstract to the concrete. (See chapter 4.)

Journal Writing

Although writing is an individual act, discussing and brainstorming activities using cooperative learning will generate ideas for journal writing and provide encouragement for students who need assistance.

In guiding students to write in their journals about the field trip, urge them to rely on their senses:

- How did the seashore smell?
- How did the texture of the bark of a tree feel?
- How quiet was it in the forest?
- How did you feel when you first saw the (statue, animal, ocean)?

Encourage them to write about not just the what but the how and why of events:

- How did the journey to the field trip site begin?
- Why is the building in the center of the city?
- What did you observe on the way?
- Would you like to be a guard at the museum?
- What would it be like to decide which painting the museum purchases?
- How do you become a park ranger?

Provide a relaxed atmosphere for writing. You may want to create a writer's corner with pillows. Help students get in the frame of mind to write by talking with them about relaxing, closing their eyes, and looking at the pictures they see in their heads. Play a musical tape as the writing time begins. Setting the tone with classical music may soon become a habit. Ask students to suggest composers or music that they enjoy. The only requirement for the music is that it should be without lyrics.

Adding Illustrations

As mentioned earlier, drawings, clippings from magazines, postcards, and portions of brochures add an extra creative dimension to journal writing. Vera B. Williams' *Stringbean's Trip to the Shining Sea* (1988) and *Three Days on a River in a Red Canoe* (1981) can be used as fictional journal writing models that include illustrations. The former describes the wonderful adventures of Stringbean Coe and his big brother, Fred, as they travel from Jeloway, Kansas, to the Pacific Ocean. Postcards and photographs are shown in an album format and are complete with varying addresses and with messages that are childlike. The "stamps" on the postcards offer readers humorous details. The latter book portrays two cousins and their mothers who all pool their money to purchase a red canoe and take a weekend trip on the river, which provides an exciting adventure. The activities of building camp fires, cooking, (recipes are included), observing wild animals, and coping with the elements of weather are intriguing.

For students who insist that they cannot draw, use examples from James Thurber, and simple line drawings to illustrate that drawings do not need to be filled with detail to enhance the writing. Compare specific illustrations of trees, animals, and houses from Caldecott Award books, emphasizing that there is no "right" way to draw any of these objects. A drawing is the artist's interpretation of an object or experience.

Models for Journal Writing

Students may not be familiar with diaries or journals. Try to provide them with examples. In her book *Marco Polo: His Notebook* (1990), Susan L. Roth uses the journal format just as Marco Polo might have used it in writing his own journal. The author combines old photographs and maps to create a splendid model of journal writing for young people. Older students can be introduced to *Diary of a Young Girl* by Anne Frank (1952), which is a terrific example of a young girl recording her feelings and descriptions of relationships.

If a student would like to write a journal from the viewpoint of an animal, Robert Lawson's book *Ben and Me: A New and Astonishing Life of Benjamin Franklin as Written by His Good Mouse Amos* (1939) is an excellent example. Suggest that if students have a pet (cat, gerbil, rabbit) they can consider how that animal would have reported the field trip if they had been in the student's pocket or knapsack. The journal entries for one week will be "reported" by the animal.

An example of a historical journal is Margaret Wise Brown's *Homes in the Wilderness: A Pilgrim's Journal of Plymouth Plantation in 1620* (1939). This text is modernized and is from a journal first published in London in 1622 and believed to have been written by Governor Bradford and others of the Mayflower company.

The book *Imagine* (1990), by Alison Lester, is an excellent book to use in practicing imaginative situations. The double-page illustrations surrounded with words of objects or animals found in the picture can be used as a model for beginning writing activities.

Journal Writing in Kindergarten

It is never too early to begin the writing journey. In *Multiple Worlds of Child Writers: Friends Learning To Write* (1989), Anne Haas Dyson describes monitoring kindergartners' participation in journal writing.

> Before actually beginning to write in their journals, the kindergartners often engaged in whole-class projects focused on words, especially their names, and letters. They read their own and each other's names. . . . Margaret had begun her career teaching high school students, some of whom could not read or write and who did not seem to have made the connection between their spoken ideas and the printed word. She wanted her kindergartners to be "immediately aware that these little marks on the paper have to do with the things that come out of their mouths," that is, with their expressive language. She thus asked the kindergartners to dictate "stories" to accompany their drawn pictures. In the kindergarten class, following the opening activities, children could choose what to do next, and one of the "choices" was journal writing. As noted already, the journal activity was the cornerstone of the school's literacy program. It was meant as a way for children to express their own experiences and feelings with the school. Since their own written thoughts would be read, the journal activity was viewed by the school faculty as both a reading and a

writing activity and as one that would be meaningful to children from a variety of backgrounds.

Other Writing Activities

PMI

Writing activities can be based on Edward De Bono's PMI activities (1982). He suggests posing a question such as "Should all bicycles be painted yellow?" to the class. Such questioning gives students the opportunity to express their personal views, and it demonstrates that not all questions have a right or a wrong answer. The students must examine each answer and designate its Plus (good) points, its Minus (negative) points, and its Interesting points. This type of activity serves as an attention-directing tool—in doing a PMI attention is first focused on the Plus points, then toward the Minus points, and finally toward the Interesting points. This deliberate and disciplined activity is completed over a period of about two to three minutes.

Practicing this activity with the class will enable students to feel free to voice opinions in their writing as well as orally. After students become comfortable voicing their own opinions, ideas, and concerns about such questions, you can move on to other topics.

Examples of possible PMI topics include

- The idea of a zoo as a part of the school grounds
- Conducting school every day at the seashore
- Using the museum as a school

Research Paper Alternatives

Alternative approaches to research paper writing formed the basis of a paper presented by Gaynell M. Fuchs (1987) at the Spring Conference of the National Council of Teachers of English. The paper explained a project in which students, following a field trip to the Honolulu Academy of Arts and a background survey of library materials, were assigned to write about a reproduction of an artwork that included an image of a woman. They could either assume the identity of the woman in the artwork and discuss her life and background, or they could assume the role of museum docent and explain the woman and the artwork to a group of museum visitors.

Fuchs felt that this addition of "voice," or point of view, added a freshness of expression to student writing. She also found that

- There was little evidence of plagiarism
- Students expanded on the topic as they became interested
- From the standpoint of fostering writing as thinking, there was a much better synthesis of material
- Students seemed better able to grasp the actual role of the woman in her society as they identified with her

Fuchs also cited the essential step of planning with the librarian for adequate resources. For a research project like this one, students would require information on periods of history, art history, costume, fashion, jewelry, women's studies, social history, weddings, and marriage customs.

If a field trip is not possible to view original art, students can base their research papers on reproductions of paintings. A field trip to an art museum will, however, give them a better appreciation for original art. After viewing an original in a museum, the reproduction, like a photograph, can be used to refresh their memories. Students will be surprised at how the size of the original work of art compares to that of the reproduction and how the use of color and light varies between them. This research writing activity should suggest other, more simplified, writing activities based on field trips to art museums. (See appendix B for a complete description of Fuchs' Women in Art project.)

Combining Timelines and Writing Activities

Architecture, history, writing, and field trips can be combined to teach students about local or national history. Both the exteriors and interiors of buildings hold historic significance and provide opportunities for students to improve their visual skills. Observing architecture, students will come to appreciate the changes in style and technology. Their observations can be combined with a timeline to give students a framework for understanding the sequence of history.

R. Anne Dilworth (Arlington Public Schools), in a project supported by a grant from the National Endowment for the Humanities, designed a teaching unit for eleventh grade United States history students. Although it was based on the nation's government buildings, any public building could be used. Students began the project by defining the word "building," then they identified, drew, evaluated, and described buildings that were familiar to them. A timeline was developed to show historical events in relation to the dates that public buildings were being erected. The students used the textbook, pamphlets, and other reference sources as they gathered data about the architecture of the United States Capitol. Transparencies and slides provided details about columns, the dome, pediments, and the balustrade. Additional instruction included a film on the city of Washington, D.C., to enable students to see the building prior to the field trip. On the trip the students completed an Architecture Task Worksheet, which included identification of buildings near the Capitol. Dilworth suggested that this unit could be adapted to be used with

1. Ancient or World History Class—to show the connection and influence of Classical Greece and Rome on later time periods in history, especially 1790–1820 in Europe and the United States.
2. American History/Government Class—to show how founders of this nation drew on Classical Rome and Greece, not only for political ideas, but also for architectural styles which they felt would benefit the nation's Capitol.
3. Latin Class—to illustrate and reflect upon the long lasting contributions of the Romans in the areas of architecture and government.
4. Photography class—how to photograph buildings, parts of buildings, photograph specific style of architecture, to do a picture story of the Capitol and what transpires there daily. Photograph peoples' reactions to the Capitol when they first see it.

"The unit includes lesson descriptions, suggested materials, quizzes, homework assignments, a sample timeline, architectural handouts, bulletin board displays, sketches, floor plans, maps, and a field trip schedule." (This 68-page guide is available for $2.50 from Arlington Public Schools, 1426 N. Quincy Street, Arlington, VA 22207, or ERIC document ED 239 954.)

Writing across the Curriculum

Writing across the curriculum can give students opportunities to see the interrelatedness of all aspects of learning. Many simulation games support such writing activities. In one project entitled *Pioneers*, elementary school students explored the problems and decisions faced by early pioneers on a wagon train and later compared them to problems that will face future space pioneers (Mielke 1988). After the students were divided into four wagon train groups, each student was given a *Pioneers* handbook, describing the type of character they were to role play and information on the household items, foods, tools, miscellaneous supplies, and personal items that they had to decide to take or leave behind. A trail map (patterned after the Oregon and California Trails) was created on butcher paper, and the students drew fate cards with events that might have occurred along the trail. As students made plans and decisions about their simulated wagon train journey, they kept a diary about their journey. Once the simulated journey was over, the students could refer to their handbooks for research paper guidelines; all of the topics included related to the history of the West. Students completed the three week project with a better understanding of the dangers that faced early settlers, improved research skills, and experience in cooperative learning and decision making.

Additional ideas for incorporating writing throughout the curriculum and, specifically, into field trip activities are presented by Hilarie N. Staton in *The Content Connection: How To Integrate Thinking and Writing in the Content Areas* (1991). Each page begins with "Think & Organize" and concludes with "Write." The author describes ways to weave fiction into factual reporting, how to write "fillers" used in the newspaper, and how to create "If . . . then" stories based on history.

Cooperative Learning

The use of cooperative learning techniques throughout the field trip experience will provide students with opportunities for positive interdependence, improvement of social skills, and group processing. Effectiveness of cooperative learning—as opposed to competitive learning—and its benefits to students are supported by research that has been conducted throughout the past fifty years. These studies indicate that, when used properly, cooperative learning will improve academic achievement, social skills, and student self-esteem. Implementation of cooperative learning changes the role of the teacher from that of sole conveyor of knowledge to that of "guide of learning events or . . . resource person" (Manning and Lucking 1991), creating an environment that allows students to learn from each other. The skills that students acquire in cooperating, rather than in competing, will, in turn, enhance future field trips and follow-up writing experiences.

Much has been written about the topic of cooperative learning. Following are some excellent sources for extending your knowledge on this subject:

- Cooperative learning is the focus of the December 1989/January 1990 issue of *Educational Leadership*
- *Leading the Cooperative School* (1989), by David W. and Roger T. Johnson, reports on 25 years of theory, research, and practical experience in cooperative learning
- "The What, Why, and How of Cooperative Learning," written by M. Lee Manning and Robert Lucking (1991), is another excellent overview

Conclusion

As a concluding exercise, rethink the objectives outlined when the trip was planned. A discussion with students can provide information about the learning that took place as a result of the trip. List the positive effects and any negative ones. If the objectives were not met, discuss whether they were realistic. Were they vague, overambitious, or inappropriate? Also ask chaperones for their opinions about the success of the trip, and incorporate their identification of problems and their suggestions into future planning.

Continue to write and plan for the next field trip. As new books are added to the library, consider whether they would enhance a field trip or provide ideas for future destinations. Develop a field trip bibliography; it will save time in planning future trips and will also assist students with their research and response to the trips.

Field trips involve detailed planning. They can be tiring, and they can be filled with unexpected opportunities for learning not encountered in the classroom. As you consider the positives and negatives of the field trip, make plans to discuss, with your students, the year's field trips on the last day of school. Do students remember events of each trip? Have they retained what they learned? If the answers are yes, you already have the beginnings of answers to these two questions: (1) How many field trips must I plan for the next school year? and (2) When do we leave?

Reading, writing, and field experience: the combination of these three factors can provide students with lifelong memories and a knowledge base for moving into higher-order thinking skills. The challenge of planning and completing a successful field trip offers too many learning experiences to be ignored.

Appendix A:
Sample Forms and Lists

Recommendations for School Board
Field Trip Policies

The key to minimizing risk on field trips is providing adequate supervision. Legally and morally, adequate supervision means whatever supervision you need to avoid injury or harm that reasonably could have been foreseen and prevented. The age of the students involved and the potential hazards of the trip determine how many chaperons you need. Use a permission slip to let parents know the possible risks their children run in participating in a field trip and what safeguards you will take to minimize those risks. But don't assume a signed permission slip eliminates your liability should an accident occur: you still must provide adequate and responsible supervision during the field trip. (Chandler 1985)

Formulation of School District Policies for Field Trips

I. Board should frame policies that encourage opportunities for students to have experiences that cannot be duplicated within the classroom

II. Objectives for field trip should
    A. Indicate how trip meshes with curriculum
    B. Explain what follow-up activities are planned
    C. Outline educational value to students

III. Field trip sites should be screened/approved for suitability and value

IV. All students should be afforded access to this educational opportunity, not denied because of the idiosyncratic considerations of one teacher or principal

V. Each grade level should identify field trip sites, approved by a majority of teachers on the grade level, as
    A. Essential
    B. Desirable

VI. The field trip list should be evaluated annually by representatives of all grade levels to avoid duplication

VII. The list of approved field trips should include
    A. Contact person at field trip site
        1. Name
        2. Address
        3. Telephone number
    B. Map indicating location of site to be visited
    C. List of possible hazards and safeguards
    D. Estimated cost
    E. Ratio of chaperons to students
    F. Learner outcome for students
    G. Correlation of field trip to curriculum

VIII. Provision for school buses and drivers

IX. Permission form to be signed by each student's parent or guardian prior to the trip

X. Insurance coverage

XI. Procedures to be followed in the event of an emergency
    A. Authorization for emergency medical treatment
    B. Person responsible for notifying parents and school officials in the event of an emergency

XII. Procedure for approval of proposed field trip

XIII. Who is responsible for providing adequate supervision

XIV. Duties and responsibilities of chaperons

Administrative procedures should include information on the following:
    Costs of field trips
    Transportation
    Provision for students who are unable to pay
    Deadline for requesting permission/receipt of permission forms

---

Request for School Bus Field Trips

REQUEST ROUTING: 1. Building Principal   2. Transportation   3. Business Office

REQUEST FROM: Employee's Name _____

School _____

Date of Request _____   Date of Trip _____

Departure Time _____   Return Time _____

Grade Level _____   Number of Students _____

Point of Origin _____

Destination _____
(Place, Street, and City)

Student Group _____
(Social Studies, Industrial Arts, etc.)

Request To Eat on Trip _____
(Name and Location)

Educational Purpose of Trip _____

Chaperones _____

I have reviewed this request and certify that this proposed trip conforms with the policies of the board of education. I recommend that approval be granted.

Requested by: _____   Principal: _____

Approved: Yes   No   Approved: Yes   No
Comments: _____   Comments: _____

_____   _____

_____   _____
Business Manager   Transportation Supervisor

Teachers' and Coaches' Responsibilities

1. Provide specific location of destination on this request form so that bus driver may plan route to travel.
2. Buses are not available before _____ and must be back at the bus garage by _____ when school is in session.
3. Field trips are limited to _____ buses per day for the school district.
4. Allow _____ working days for processing of bus request.
5. Maintain student discipline while enroute to and from field trips.
6. Leave the bus clean.
7. Notify the transportation department as soon as possible if the field trip is to be cancelled.
8. No field trips are to be scheduled for the first _____ weeks or the last _____ weeks of school.

Trip Evaluation

GROUP SUPERVISOR		Yes	No
1.	Was bus on time?		
2.	Was driver courteous?		
3.	Was bus operated safely?		
4.	Was driver cooperative?		
COMMENTS:			

BUS DRIVER		Yes	No
1.	Was group ready to start at time requested?		
2.	Were regulations followed?		
3.	Was group prompt in loading for return trip?		
4.	Was supervision satisfactory?		
COMMENTS:			

Emergency Medical Authorization

Student Name: _____

Address: _____

Telephone: _____

School Attended: _____

Parent or Guardian: _____

Purpose—to enable parents to authorize emergency treatment for children who become ill or injured while under school authority, when parents cannot be reached.

PART I OR PART II MUST BE COMPLETED

Part I (TO GRANT REQUEST)

In the event reasonable attempts to contact me at _____(phone number) or other parent at _____(phone number) have been unsuccessful, I hereby give my consent for (1) the administration of any treatment deemed necessary by Dr. _____(preferred physician) or Dr._____ (preferred dentist), or, in the event the designated preferred practitioner is not available, by another licensed physician or dentist; and (2) the transfer of the child to_____ (preferred hospital) or any hospital reasonably accessible.

   This authorization does not cover major surgery unless the medical opinions of two other licensed physicians or dentists, concurring in the necessity for such surgery, are obtained before surgery is performed.

   Facts concerning the child's medical history including allergies, medications being taken, and any physical impairments to which a physician should be alerted: _____
_____
_____
_____

Date _____   Signature of Parent _____
                    Address _____

DO NOT COMPLETE PART II IF YOU COMPLETED PART I

Part II (REFUSAL TO CONSENT)

I do NOT give my consent for emergency medical treatment of my child. In the event of illness or injury requiring medical treatment, I wish the school authorities to take no action or to do the following: _____

_____

_____

_____

_____

_____

Date _____ Signature of Parent _____

Address _____

Parental Acknowledgment Form
for Extended Trips

In giving permission for _____
to take part in the proposed trip to _____,
to be led by _____ , as chaperone,
I understand and acknowledge that this trip is not approved or sponsored
by the Board of Education of the School District and that_____
is acting in his capacity as a private individual and not in any way as an
employee of the Board of Education. I further understand that the Board
of Education assumes no responsibility for such unapproved trips.

Parent or Guardian _____

Date _____

Sample Objectives and Activities
for a Field Trip

The following was taken from the Aims film "A Magical Field Trip to the Dinosaur Museum," a 15-minute video for primary and intermediate age groups, produced by Field Trip Videos, Aims Media, 6901 Woodley Avenue, Van Nuys, CA 91406-4878.

Objectives:

- To understand the process involved in reconstructing dinosaur skeletons from fossils
- To recognize that fossils are principally found in sedimentary rocks
- To develop an awareness of the necessity of using specific tools to complete the job
- To understand that scientists use clues to study, classify, and organize the fossils
- To stimulate curiosity and the quest for learning more about fossils and dinosaurs through enrichment activities and provocative questions

Vocabulary:

carnivore, eroded, exhibits, exposing, fossil, fragile, minerals, museum, paleontologist, plaster, rock, sedimentary, seeped, site, skeletons

Questions and Activities:

What stories have you read about dinosaurs?

Has anyone ever seen a live dinosaur? Why not?

How do you think we know that there were such animals as dinosaurs?

What are duties of a paleontologist? Would you like this type of job? Why or why not?

Describe how a fossil is created.

Why is it important for a paleontologist to wear goggles when he or she is digging for fossils?

What do they do at the museum if they can't find all of the bones for a certain dinosaur skeleton?

How does a paleontologist determine the size of each dinosaur?

Name some animals that are not extinct that in some way remind you of the dinosaurs. Why?

What is the difference between a carnivore and a herbivore? Create a chart listing which dinosaurs were carnivores and which were herbivores.

Design your own dinosaur exhibit. Choose one type of dinosaur. Find out about its environment. Make a diorama showing that dinosaur in its environment.

Fossils can be found in sedimentary rock. What are some specific types of sedimentary rock? Collect some samples and label them. Display for class.

Compare a picture of a human skeleton to that of a dinosaur skeleton. List some ways they are the same, different.

What does the word extinct mean? What if the dinosaurs had not become extinct? Write a description of what the world would be like at the present time if dinosaurs were still around.

Conduct a survey at your school to find the best liked dinosaur. Create a bar graph to show results.

What other animals are in danger of becoming extinct? Choose one and write an editorial explaining what should be done to protect this animal. . . .Why?

What is the Loch Ness monster? Make a drawing of what it supposedly looks like. Compare to pictures of dinosaurs. How is it alike, different?

Invent a dinosaur of your own. Name it. What does it eat, how does it move, where does it live? Write a description and illustrate.

Find out why dinosaurs became extinct. Justify your answer.

Brainstorm (class) as many words as you can about dinosaurs. Write a poem.

Choose a favorite, write a report, make a model, clay or papier-mâché.

Did some dinosaurs fly? Did some live in water, land? Make a chart, categorizing your information.

Create your own fossil imprint. Cut the top off a half pint milk carton. Completely cover some small shells with Vaseline. Pour some plaster of Paris into milk carton. Very quickly place shells on top of plaster. Gently press shells into plaster. After plaster has dried, carefully remove shells and tear away the milk carton.

Invite a paleontologist to class.

Contact a rock collector. Bring samples of fossils to class.

Have a geologist come to class. Ask about formation of igneous, sedimentary, and metamorphic rocks. Describe where sedimentary rock can be found.

Checklist: Should I Take This Trip?

Yes   No   1. Will this field trip aid in clarification of concepts suggested in the classroom?

Yes   No   2. Can the experience of the field trip be infused into the curriculum?

Yes   No   3. Will the field trip be supported by staff, administration and parents?

Yes   No   4. Will a field trip help correct misconceptions (i.e. interrelationships and factual content) through direct observation?

Yes   No   5. Will a field trip be worth the expenditure of time, money, and effort?

Yes   No   6. Is there a facility at the proposed site that will contribute to the accomplishment of the instructional objectives?

Yes   No   7. Will a field trip serve to accomplish objectives more thoroughly than if representatives went and reported back to the class?

Yes   No   8. Will it be more effective to invite a resource person or show a videotape than to undertake the field trip?

Yes   No   9. Will the trip provide an adequate sampling or desirable factors or processes to meet the instructional objectives?

Yes   No 10. Will the field trip be valuable to other factors that are discrete to the particular unit or focus of study?

Number of YES answers _____

Number of NO answers _____

Should I take this field trip? _____

Reprinted with permission from Edward J. Zielinski. "So You Want To Take a Field Trip," 1987. ED 299 079.

Water Use Tally Sheet

	Number of Times Each Day				Amount of Water Each Time	Total Use
	1	2	3	Total		
Personal						
Wash hands						
Brush teeth						
Flush toilet						
Drinking water						
Bath/Shower						
Household						
Wash dishes						
Wash clothes						
Cooking						
Water plants						
Spinkle lawn						
Wash car						
Cleaning						
Recreational						
Swimming						
Boating						
Fishing						
Water skiing						

Adapted from "Our World of Water: A Spring Program for Fifth Graders." Washington, DC: Dahlem Environmental Education Center, Jackson Community College, 1983. ED 249 112.

Animal Observation Fact Sheet

Field trip site:_____ **Date:** _____

Common name for animal:

Scientific name:

Description of habitat:

How the animal moves:
- ☐ Walk _____
- ☐ Run _____
- ☐ Crawl _____
- ☐ Swim _____
- ☐ Fly _____

Body description:

Head:
- ☐ Ears (floppy, slick, fur-covered, pointed) _____
- ☐ Eyes (shape, location) _____
- ☐ Nose (size, shape) _____
- ☐ Mouth (size, shape) _____
- ☐ Teeth (shape, sharp, flat) _____

Body covered by:
- ☐ Fur (color, texture, condition) _____
- ☐ Skin (color, texture) _____
- ☐ Scales (color, texture, pattern) _____
- ☐ Other (describe) _____

Tail:

- ☐ Long, short, covered with _____
- ☐ Shape _____
- ☐ Special purpose _____

Behavior:

Feeding:

- ☐ Type of food _____

Activities:

- ☐ Running, pacing, grooming _____

Noises:

- ☐ Types of sounds _____

Comments: _____

_____

_____

Adapted from James L. Milson. "Data Sheet for Animal Observation." In "Looking Around at the Zoo." *Science and Children* 21 (February 1984): 24–27.

Checklist for an *Imaginary* Trip to a Foreign Country

☐ Passport application (get from government office)
☐ Form for immunization record
☐ Immunization record

The following immunizations are required for entry into
_____ *(name of country)*

☐ Cholera
☐ Diphtheria
☐ Measles
☐ Mumps
☐ Pertussis
☐ Polio
☐ Rubella
☐ Tetanus
☐ Yellow Fever

Students may request that the school nurse visit the classrooms to discuss the reasons for immunizations and the cause and effects of some of the diseases.

Research in the library will provide an opportunity to use almanacs to determine incidence of disease and deaths in various countries. Preventative health measures can also be researched.

Teacher's Checklist for Planning a Field Trip

☐ 1. Goals/objectives for the field trip
☐ 2. Selection of field trip site
☐ 3. Visit to the site
☐ 4. Selection of field trip date
☐ 5. Approval by school district
☐ 6. Transportation arrangements
☐ 7. Bulletin board display
☐ 8. Vocabulary list
☐ 9. Arrangement for chaperones
☐ 10. Pre–field trip instructional activities
☐ 11. Distribution of student checklist of items needed for trip
☐ 12. Distribution of permission slips
☐ 13. Review of schedule of events with students
☐ 14. Review of activities to be completed at the site
☐ 15. Discussion of field trip rules
☐ 16. Post–field trip activities
☐ 17. Evaluation of field trip

Adapted from John Pauls. "Marine Biology Field Trip Sites: Ocean Related Curriculum Activities." Seattle, WA: Pacific Science Center/Sea Grant Marine Education Project, 1980. ED 289-681.

Student Field Trip Checklist

Necessary for the field trip to _____

☐ Permission slip

☐ Time schedule for the field trip

☐ Lunch or lunch money

☐ Pen/pencil

☐ Writing materials

☐ Small amount of money (if necessary) for trip to museum shop

☐ Medication

☐ Camera or tape recorder

☐ Jacket, hat, gloves, raincoat

☐ Knapsack

(Other items may be added to the checklist depending on the site, weather, distance, objectives.)

Things we will not need on the trip

☐ Expensive jewelry

☐ Large sums of money

(Add additional items as needed.)

Sample Field Trip Rules

The field trip destination is considered an extension of our school. All school rules will apply. Rules for conduct are outlined in the school handbook.

1. We will not be the only visitors to the field trip site. Be certain that you do not interfere with others who wish to enjoy their visit to this site.

2. Be cautious. If we are out of doors, be certain that you follow the marked paths. If we are indoors, use the stair railing. We do not run in the halls at school, nor will we run on the field trip.

3. If you want to explore an area not on our map, be certain that you take an adult with you.

4. If we are in an outdoor area, be certain that we leave the area in the same condition we found it.

5. Shoes are a must, both inside and out.

6. If you do not feel well, please quickly tell the teacher or chaperone.

7. Additional rules for certain field trips: (to be added as needed due to building or district rules)

Sample Letter to Parents

Dear Parent/Guardian,

Our class will be taking a field trip to _____
This trip is a part of our study of _____
At the _____ we plan to continue our study by visiting
_____, viewing exhibits of _____,
and answering the questions developed in a class discussion.

We feel that you will want to use this opportunity to build on this educational
experience for your child. This will be an excellent opportunity for you to
plan a follow-up visit to _____.

You may want to consider:

- A visit to the public library to assist with research on this topic
- Encouraging your child to write a letter to a relative about the field trip
- Listening to your child relate experiences of the field trip and asking open-ended questions such as:

    How did you feel when you saw _____?
    Why do you think _____?
    How could you improve _____?

Thanks for your support.

Sincerely,

_____ Grade Teacher

Sample Schedule

Schedule for field trip to _____

Date _____

_____ a.m.   Arrive at school; review student checklist

_____ a.m.   Depart from school

_____ a.m.   Arrive at field trip site

_____ a.m.   Orientation to the site; questions and answers

_____ a.m.   Regroup; answer questions; set place to meet for lunch

_____ a.m.   Lunch

_____ p.m.   Discuss activities of a.m.; reaffirm time schedule for afternoon

_____ p.m.   Gather at _____(location) for return trip

_____ p.m.   Board bus for return trip

_____ p.m.   Arrive at school

Appendix B:
Women in Art
Research Project Guide

Introduction

Darwin: "Each race tends to admire those characteristics that are unique to it and distinguish it from others."

Voltaire: "Beauty is often relative . . . what is decent in Japan is quite indecent in Rome and what is fashionable in Paris is not so in Peking."

Schopenhauer: "Behind each man's sexual impulse, compelling him toward the propagation of the species[,] is his basic sense of beauty."

Assumption: Beauty is in the eye of the beholder and the idea of beauty or what is beautiful varies from time to time and from place to place.

The Project

Using a specific work of art, you will attempt to understand what the woman in your painting or sculpture represents in terms of the cultural values of her day.

The Procedure

1. Choose a work of art which appeals to you from the reproductions on display.

2. Determine the time period, the culture or country of the woman, and make a guess at the social class she represents. (The title of the painting and how she is portrayed are good clues to this.) Then, fill out the Criticism Worksheet. You must complete the Description and Analysis sections *before* you begin your research. You may wish to do the Interpretation section later.

3. To begin your research, check the bibliography provided for you and then choose appropriate books.

4. Do some reading on the time period of your painting. You will need to find sources that discuss the life of a woman during the time period your picture represents, as well as sources that discuss costume. As you read, take notes. Think of such questions as: What would this woman do each day? Would she be in a position of power or be acted upon by others? What sort of education would she have received? How hard would she work to survive? Is she dependent on others? When might she marry and how? What sort of role would she play at home and away from it? What might she do for amusement? What kind of clothing is she wearing? What sort of makeup, jewelry, and hairstyle? What does her costume say about her life style and what is expected of her? Can she move freely? Is she covered up or does her flesh show?

   Gather information to produce an understanding of the woman's life. As you take notes, put the material in your own words. Do not copy directly from your sources. Be sure to include the page number and a key on each of your note cards. (Note cards will be handed in. You may xerox material to work on at home; however, xerox material will not be accepted as notes. Notes must be in your own words!)

5. Write a rough draft, choosing one of the following methods:

   a. Role play the woman. You are the woman in the painting. Using material you have read about the life and costume of "your" day, write about yourself as if you were keeping a diary or writing a letter to a friend or relative. Your task is to apply your research materials to a creative description of "your" life.

   b. If being a woman bothers you, then you may take the identity of someone close to her such as a brother, husband, father, fiance. Write in journal or letter form. Again, you will be incorporating facts into a fictitious life.

   c. Discuss the painting as if you were an art critic. In this case, you might wish to do some additional reading on the artist or the style of art which is represented. Talk about the painting, what it represents in terms of culture, class, costume, and aesthetic concepts. Do not attempt this option unless you have a good background in art.

   You do not need to footnote, but you will turn in a bibliography and note cards.

6. Ask a friend to read your rough draft, and comment on your paper.

7. Finish the last part of your Analysis sheet (your interpretation and judgment of the painting).

8. Write your final copy. If at all possible, type it. Hand it in with note cards, the criticism worksheet, and a bibliography. The project is due on: _____.

   If you are absent, have a parent or someone bring the paper to me. Late work will not be graded. Remember, you MUST write your paper using one of the options above. I will not accept a "straight" research paper format.

Conclusion

There are several reasons for asking you to do such a project: First, and most obvious, is the opportunity to work with a research-oriented writing assignment. You are not expected to produce new knowledge, but you are expected to synthesize the facts you have read and to produce a well-organized paper. I am more interested in having you read and put together information than I am in making you search for materials. That is why a bibliography has been prepared for you. [Note: The bibliography included in Ms. Fuch's document is not included. A bibliography must be a combined effort of the teacher and school librarian and will be unique to that library collection.]

Second, I hope that you will gain an understanding of human beings and their relationship to the world during a specific period of time. You should have an awareness of that particular time and culture which is in greater depth than you had when you started the project. You may begin to ask questions about how this time period differs from your own culture, and hopefully, be inspired to read more widely about other cultures and times in order to understand your own.

Third, I hope you will gain some appreciation of visual art and the very important role it has played in the world. This is an opportunity to broaden your understanding of this medium of communication, and I hope, this project will make our life richer and more meaningful. That, after all, is the object of education.

Criticism Worksheet

Title of work: _____

Artist: _____

Date of work: _____

Country: _____

Description: (List everything you see in the picture, describing it as fully as you can.)

Analysis: (List questions which you will have to address to understand this woman's role.)

Interpretation and judgment: (What, to you, is the meaning, mood, idea of this work of art? How does it make you feel?)

Research Paper Time Table

Day One: Read the handout for homework. Buy 4 x 6 note cards and bring them to the library. If possible, go to _____ and look at the reproductions on display. Choose one or two reproductions that appeal to you.

Day Two: Listening/Viewing area. Picture Appraisal Practice. I will demonstrate how to do the Criticism worksheet, and then you will have some time to find a painting of your own. The librarian and I will also explain the location of materials and how to use the bibliography efficiently. [Note: The bibliography provided by Ms. Fuchs is not included in the index.]

Day Three: Sign in and choose a carrel. Select a book and take notes. Number your sources and put this number key on each note card. Limit information on a card to one subject. Each card should have: (1). heading (2). key (3). page number (4). information in your own words. As you use a book, make a bibliography card and save these for doing the bibliography.

Day 4–6: Continue taking notes. By day 5 you should be ready to start a rough draft. Check to see if you need more materials.

You will have additional time to work on your own before the paper is due. Materials will remain on reserve in _____ for at least one additional week.

Note: Research materials are on reserve. This means they cannot be removed from the library at any time. There will be no exceptions to this rule. If you wish to find additional information in other libraries, please feel free to do so.

All materials in appendix B reprinted with permission from Gaynell M. Fuchs. "Mona Lisa Writes a Letter: An Alternative to the Research Paper," 1987. ERIC Document 282194.

Appendix C: Phone Numbers for State Geological Surveys

Educational goals will vary from state to state. Write to your state geological survey office to determine the scope of their educational program. Ask for a list of publications.

Alabama. . . . . (205) 349-2852
Alaska . . . . (907) 474-7147
Arizona . . . . (602) 621-7906
Arkansas . . . . (501) 371-1488
California. . . . . (916) 445-1923
Colorado . . . . (303) 866-2611
Connecticut . . . . (203) 566-3540
Delaware . . . . (302) 451-2833
Florida . . . . (904) 488-4191
Georgia . . . . (404) 656-3214
Hawaii . . . . (808) 548-7539
Idaho . . . . (208) 885-7991
Illinois . . . . (217) 344-1481
Indiana. . . . . (812) 335-2863

Iowa	(319) 338-1173
Kansas	(913) 864-3965
Kentucky	(606) 257-5863
Louisiana	(504) 342-6754
Maine	(207) 289-2801
Maryland	(301) 338-7066
Massachusetts	(617) 292-5690
Michigan	(517) 373-1256
Minnesota	(612) 373-3372
Mississippi	(601) 354-6228
Missouri	(314) 364-1752
Montana	(406) 496-4166
Nebraska	(402) 472-3471
Nevada	(702) 784-6691
New Hampshire	(603) 862-1216
New Jersey	(609) 292-2576
New Mexico	(505) 835-5420
New York	(518) 474-5816
North Carolina	(919) 733-3833
North Dakota	(701) 777-2231
Ohio	(614) 265-6605
Oklahoma	(405) 325-3031
Oregon	(503) 229-5580
Pennsylvania	(717) 787-2169
Puerto Rico	(809) 723-2716
Rhode Island	(401) 277-2656
South Carolina	(803) 758-6431
South Dakota	(605) 624-4471
Tennessee	(615) 742-6689
Texas	(512) 471-1534
Utah	(801) 581-6831
Vermont	(802) 828-3365
Virginia	(804) 293-5121
Washington	(206) 459-6372
West Virginia	(304) 594-2331
Wisconsin	(608) 262-1705
Wyoming	(307) 766-2286

Appendix D:
Books about Zoos

Bahr, Robert. *Blizzard at the Zoo*. New York: Lothrop, Lee & Shepard, 1982.

Cajacob, Thomas. *Close to the Wild: Siberian Tigers in a Zoo*. New York: Carolrhoda, 1986.

Gibbons, Gail. *Zoo*. New York: Crowell, 1987.

Grosvenor, Donna K. *Zoo Babies*. Washington, DC: National Geographic Society, 1978.

Hewett, John. *Watching Them Grow: Inside a Zoo Nursery*. Boston: Little, Brown, 1979.

Hoban, Tana. *A Children's Zoo*. New York: Greenwillow, 1985.

Hoffmeister, Donald. *Zoo Animals*. Chicago: Golden Press, 1967.

Johnston, Ginny. *Andy Bear: A Polar Cub Grows Up at the Zoo*. New York: Morrow, 1985.

Lerner, Mark. *Career at a Zoo*. New York: Lerner, 1980.

National Zoological Park. *Zoobook*. Washington, DC: Smithsonian Institution Press, 1976.

Rinard, Judith E. *What Happens at the Zoo*. Washington, DC: National Geographic Society, 1984.

———. *Zoos without Cages*. Washington, DC: National Geographic Society, 1981.

Thompson, Peggy. *Keepers and Creatures at the National Zoo*. New York: Crowell, 1988.

Bibliography

Aeschylus. *Prometheus Bound.* Translated by James Scully and John C. Herington. New York: Oxford University Press, 1990.

Anderson, Connie. "Adventure." *People* 9 (June 5, 1978): 72–74.

Arnosky, Jim. *Drawing from Nature.* New York: Lothrop, Lee & Shepard, 1982.

Asimov, Isaac. *Biographical Encyclopedia of Science and Technology: The Lives and Achievements of 1510 Great Scientists from Ancient Times to the Present Chronologically Arranged.* 2d ed. New York: Doubleday, 1982.

Benegar, John. *Teaching Writing Skills: A Global Approach.* Denver: Center for Teaching International Relations, 1986.

Berliner, David, and Ursula Casanova Pinero. "The Field Trip: Frill or Essential?" *Instructor* 94 (May 1985): 14–15.

Bode, Barbara A. "Dialogue Journal Writing." *The Reading Teacher* 42 (April 1989): 568–571.

Brewster, Marty. "Ten Ways To Revive Tired Learning Logs." *English Journal* 77 (February 1988): 57.

Brown, Margaret Wise. *Homes in the Wilderness: A Pilgrim's Journal of Plymouth Plantation in 1620 by William Bradford and Others of the Mayflower Company.* Hamden, CT: Linnet/Shoe String, [1939] 1988.

Brown, Sherrie. "Cruisin' Cairo!" *Instructor* 98 (Nov.–Dec. 1988): 34–37.

Browning, Nancy F. "Journal Writing: One Assignment Does More Than Improve Reading, Writing, and Thinking." *Journal of Reading* 30 (October 1986): 39–44.

Bye, Edgar C. "For the Beginning Teacher: Preparation for a Field Trip." *Today's Education* 62 (January 1973) 57.

Capacchione, Lucia. *The Creative Journal for Children: A Guide for Parents, Teachers, and Counselors.* Boston: Shambhala, 1989.

Cather, Willa. *My Ántonia.* New York: Houghton Mifflin Company, 1973.

Chandler, Theodore A. "These Policy Tips Make the Most of Field Trips." *The American School Board Journal* 172 (June 1985): 30–41.

Chetelat, Frank J. "Art, Animals, and Learning." *School Arts* 85 (October 1985): 22–23.

Cleaver, Joanne Y. "Museum Adventures." *Learning* 20 (July/August 1991) 22–24.

Cochran-Smith, Marilyn. "Word Processing and Writing in Elementary Classrooms: A Critical Review of Related Literature." *Review of Educational Research* 61 (Spring 1991): 107–155.

Cullinan, Bernice E. *Literature and the Child.* 2d ed. San Diego: Harcourt Brace Jovanovich, 1989.

Dakos, Kalli Desmarteau. "What's There To Write About?" *Instructor* 97 (August 1987): 82.

De Bono, Edward. *De Bono's Thinking Course.* New York: Facts on File Publications, 1982.

De Vito, Alfred, and Gerald H. Krockover. *Creative Sciencing: Ideas and Activities for Teachers and Children.* 3d ed. Glenview, IL: Scott, Foresman and Company, 1991.

Dilworth, R. Anne. "The Capitol Experience in Washington, D.C." Arlington, VA: National Endowment for the Humanities (NEAH), September 1983. ED 239 954.

Dyson, Anne Haas. *Multiple Worlds of Child Writers: Friends Learning To Write.* New York: Teachers College Press, 1989.

"Cooperative Learning." (Issue focus) *Educational Leadership* 47 (December 1989/January 1990).

Evans, Susan Hopson. "Local History Project: Old Buildings, Young Eyes." *The American School Board Journal* 173 (January 1987): 34.

Fadiman, Clifton, and James Howard. *Empty Pages: A Search for Writing Competence in School and Society.* Belmont, CA: Fearon Pitman Publishers, Inc., in association with the Council for Basic Education, 1979.

Falk, John H., and John D. Balling. "The Field Trip Milieu: Learning and Behavior as a Function of Contextual Events." *Journal of Educational Research* 76 (Sept.–Oct. 1982): 22–28.

Fischer, Richard B. "Successful Field Trips." *Nature Study* 37 (March 1984): 24–27.

Frank, Anne. *Diary of a Young Girl.* New York: Doubleday, 1952.

Fuchs, Gaynell M. "Mona Lisa Writes a Letter: An Alternative to the Research Paper." Paper presented at the sixth Spring Conference of the National Council of Teachers of English. Louisville, KY, March 26–28, 1987.

Gagne, R. M., and R. T. White. "Memory Structures and Learning Outcomes." *Review of Educational Research* 48 (1978): 187–222.

Garbutt, Barb. "What? A Field Trip on the Playground?" *Inside-Out: Michigan Outdoor Education Association Newsletter* 5 (Spring 1983): 7.

GTE Southwest Incorporated. *The Everything Pages.* (June 1991).

Gerstenfeld, Sheldon L. *Zoo Clues: Making the Most of Your Visit to the Zoo.* New York: Viking, 1991.

Haas, Mary E. "Catch Your Class Playing Geography Games!" *Instructor* 98 (Nov.–Dec. 1988): 39.

Harte, David V. "Fine Tuning the Learning Experience: An Information Age Model for Excellence." *NASSP Bulletin.* 73 (May 1989) 96–101.

Haynes, Norris M., Mary Harris, Essie P. Knuckle, and James P. Comer. "Benefits of Structured Field Trip Activities on Performance on the Peabody Picture Vocabulary Test (PPVT) among a Group of Black Preschoolers." 1983. ED 274 461.

Healy, Jane M. *Endangered Minds: Why Our Children Don't Think.* New York: Simon and Schuster, 1990.

Harris, Theodore L., and Richard E. Hodges, eds. *A Dictionary of Reading and Related Terms.* Newark, DE: International Reading Association, 1981.

Harte, David Victor. "Fine Tuning the Learning Experience: An Information Age Model for Excellence." *NASSP Bulletin* 73 (May 1989): 96–101.

Heylar, John. "Why the GLUB Went Mobile." *American Education* 13 (August 1977): 22–26.

Holling, H. C. *Tree in the Trail.* Boston: Houghton Mifflin Company, 1942.

Hummer, Chris C. "Logging—I Wish You Would: The Family Journal." *English Journal* 77 (February 1988): 51.

Johnson, David W., and Roger T. Johnson. *Leading the Cooperative School.* Edina, MN: Interaction Book Company, 1989.

K–6 Geography: Themes, Key Ideas, and Learning Opportunities. Washington, DC: Geographic Education National Implementation Project (GENIP) in association with Rand McNally & Company, 1987.

Kane, Joseph Nathan. *Famous First Facts.* 4th ed. Bronx, NY: Wilson, 1982.

Katulka, Lawrence. "The Boston Massacre." *Social Science Record* 22 (Fall 1985): 44–45.

Kelly, Susan H. "Nantucket Odyssey: The Field Trip as Revitalizer." *Social Education* 42 (February 1978): 126–128.

Keown, Duane. "Let's Justify the Field Trip." *American Biology Teacher* 46 (January 1984): 43–48.

Kimmel, Margaret Mary, and Elizabeth Segel. *For Reading Out Loud! A Guide to Sharing Books with Children.* Rev. ed. New York: Dell Publishing, 1991.

Kipling, Rudyard. "The Elephant's Child." *Just So Stories.* New York: Viking, 1988.

Kirkpatrick, D. L., ed. *Twentieth-Century Children's Writers.* New York: St. Martin's, 1983.

Knapp, Clifford E., Malcolm Swan, Sonia Vogl, and Robert Vogl. *Using the Outdoors To Teach Social Studies: Grades 3–10.* Charleston, WV: ERIC Clearinghouse on Rural Education and Small Schools, 1986.

Latta, B. Dawn. "In-Process and Retrospective Journals: Putting Writers Back in Writing Processes." *English Journal* 80 (January 1991): 60–66.

Lawson, Robert. *Ben and Me: A New and Astonishing Life of Benjamin Franklin, as Written by His Good Mouse Amos.* Boston: Little, Brown, 1939.

Lee, Ernest W., and Christine F. Myers. "The Field Trip as Aesthetic Experience." *Science Teacher* 47 (April 1980): 24–25.

Lester, Alison. *Imagine.* Boston: Houghton Mifflin Company, 1990.

Levin, Elaine. "Children Meet Artists: Field Trips to Artists' Studios by Los Angeles Students." *School Arts* 76 (June 1977): 20–22.

Levin, Myrna S. "Reading, Writing, and Art." *The Reading Teacher* 42 (November 1988): 172.

Levy, Virginia K. *Let's Go to the Art Museum.* New York: Harry N. Abrams, Inc., 1988.

Lockard, Martha. "PencilTip Talents." *Writing Teacher* 4 (November 1990): 26–29.

Long, Kim. *Encyclopedia of Field Trips & Educational Destinations.* Santa Barbara, CA: ABC-CLIO, 1991.

McClure, John W. "Free Tips for Geology Trips." *The Science Teacher* 52 (October 1985): 42.

———. "The Great American Geological Field Trip." *Social Education* 25 (Feb.–Mar. 1988): 8–16.

McHugh, Jim. "Adventure." *People* 9 (June 5 1978): 72–74.

MacKenzie, Andrew A., and Richard T. White. "Fieldwork in Geography and Long-term Memory Structures." *American Educational Research Journal* 19 (Winter 1982): 623–632.

Main, Edna D. "Science and Creative Writing: A Dynamic Duo." *Science and Children* 21 (January 1984): 99–100.

Mammen, Lori. *Writing Warm-Ups: K–6.* San Antonio, TX: ECS Learning Systems, Inc., 1989.

———. *Writing Warm-Ups: 7–12.* San Antonio, TX: ECS Learning Systems, Inc., 1989.

Manning, M. Lee, and Robert Lucking. "The What, Why, and How of Cooperative Learning." *Clearing House* 64 (Jan.–Feb. 1991): 152–156.

Mason, Jack Lee. "Annotated Bibliography of Field Trip Research." *School Science and Mathematics* 80 (February 1980): 155–166.

Means, Beth, and Lindy Lindner. *Everything You Needed To Learn about Writing in High School—But. . . .* Englewood, CO: Libraries Unlimited, 1989.

Mernit, Susan. "Playing with Time: Use Your Computer to Preserve the Past with This Cross-Curricular Local History Project." *Instructor* 100 (Nov.–Dec. 1990): 78–79.

Metcalf, Fay D., and Matthew T. Downey. *Teaching Local History: Trends, Tips, and Resources.* Boulder, CO: Social Science Education Consortium, Inc., in association with ERIC Clearinghouse for Social Studies/Social Science Education, 1977.

"Michigan Natural History: A Spring Activity Packet for Fourth Grade." Jackson, MI: Jackson Community College, Michigan Dahlem Environmental Education Center, 1982. 1–44. ED 259 111.

Mielke, Nedra S. "Writing across the Curriculum as Applied in an Enrichment Classroom Setting." December 1988. 1–11. ED 306 184.

Milson, James L. "Looking Around at the Zoo." *Science and Children* 21 (February 1984): 24–27

Muse, Corey, Leigh Chiarelott, and Leonard Davidman. "Teachers' Utilization of Field Trips: Prospects and Problems." *Clearing House* 56 (November 1982): 122–126.

Noble, Trinka Hakes. *The Day Jimmy's Boa Ate the Wash.* New York: Dial, 1980.

Norton, Donna. "Using a Webbing Process To Develop Children's Literature Units." *Language Arts* 59 (April 1982): 348–352.

Olcott, Mark S. "A Field Trip to Gettysburg: A Model Experience." *The History Teacher* 10 (August 1987): 487–496.

O'Connor, David E. "Learning about the American Economy through Living Museums." *Social Education* 47 (January 1983): 40–43.

Osis, Vicki J. *Water, Water, Everywhere . . . A Guide to Marine Education in Oregon.* 2d rev. ed. Corvallis, OR: Oregon State University, Corvallis, Sea Grant College Program, 1986. ED 275 539.

"Our World of Water: A Spring Program for Fifth Graders." Jackson, MI: Jackson Commuity College, Dahlem Environmental Education Center, 1983. ED 249 112.

Pauls, John. "Marine Biology Field Trip Sites: Ocean Related Curriculum Activities." Seattle, WA: Pacific Science Center/Sea Grant Marine Education Project, 1980.

Perdue, Peggy K. *Schoolyard Science.* Glenview, IL: Scott, Foresman and Company, 1991.

Perry, Susan K. *Playing Smart: A Parent's Guide to Enriching, Offbeat Learning Activities for Ages 4–14.* Minneapolis, MN: Free Spirit Publishing, Inc., 1990.

Phillips, Kathleen C., and Barbara Steiner. *Creative Writing: A Handbook for Teaching Young People.* Littleton, CO: Libraries Unlimited, 1985.

Pioneers. A simulation game. Lakeside, CA: Interact.

Pluckrose, Henry. *Pattern.* New York: Franklin Watts, 1988.

Redleaf, Rhoda. *Open the Door Let's Explore: Neighborhood Field Trips for Young Children.* St. Paul, MN: Toys 'n Things Press, 1983.

Roth, Susan L. *Marco Polo: His Notebook.* New York: Doubleday, 1990.

Russell, Helen Ross. "Ten Minute Field Trips: Using the School Grounds To Teach." *Nature Study* 37 (March 1984): 6.

Russell, Helen Ross. *A Teacher's Guide: Ten-Minute Field Trips: Using the School Grounds for Environmental Studies.* Chicago: J. G. Ferguson Publishing Company, 1973.

Rycik, Mary Taylor. "The Lost Bus and Other Tales." *Instructor* 98 (October 1988): 109.

Salter, Richard. *Are We There Yet? Travel Games for Kids.* New York: Prince Paperbacks, 1991.

7–12 Geography: Themes, Key Ideas, and Learning Opportunities. Washington, DC: Geographic Education National Implementation Project (GENIP), Committee on 7–12 Geography, with the cooperation of Rand McNally, 1989.

Sesow, F. William, and Tom McGowan. "Take the Field Trip First." *The Social Studies* 75 (Mar.–Apr. 1984): 68–70.

Schultz, Ron. "Long Distance Learning." *Omni* 10 (September 1988): 14.

Shaffer, Carolyn, and Erica Fielder. *City Safaris: A Sierra Club Explorer's Guide to Urban Adventures for Grownups and Kids.* San Francisco: Sierra Club Books, 1987.

Simmons, John S. "Thematic Units: A Context for Journal Writing." *English Journal* 78 (January 1989): 70–72.

Southwestern Bell. *December 1991–92 Yellow Pages for Greater Dallas.*

Sperry, Armstrong. *Call It Courage.* New York: Macmillan, 1940.

Stec, Genean. *The Field Trip Handbook: A Guide to Visiting Museums.* Glenview, IL: Good Year Books, 1992.

Steiner, Barbara, and Kathleen C. Phillips. *Journal Keeping for Young People.* Englewood, CO: Teacher Ideas Press, 1991.

Staley, Rebecca R., and Frederick A. Staley. "Using the Outdoors To Teach Language Arts." Washington, DC: Office of Educational Research and Improvement, 1988. ED 294 705.

Staton, Hilarie N. *The Content Connection: How To Integrate Thinking and Writing in the Content Areas.* Glenview, IL: Good Year Books, 1991.

Stoll, Donald R., ed. *Zoobooks.* Copublished by Educational Press Association of America (New Jersey) and International Reading Association (Delaware).

Strickland, Dorothy S., and Lesley Mandel Morrow, eds. *Emerging Literacy: Young Children Learn To Read and Write.* Newark, DE: International Reading Association, 1989.

Tchudi, Susan and Stephen. *The Young Writer's Handbook: A Practical Guide for the Beginner Who Is Serious about Writing.* New York: Macmillan Publishing Company, 1984.

"Teacher's Guide to Electronic Field Trips." Instructional Support Services Division of the Board of Cooperative Educational Services, serving Chenango County and parts of Delaware, Madison, and Otsego counties in upstate New York.

Todd, Teri L. "Hitting the Road." *Instructor* 99 (March 1990): 33–34.

Van De Walle, Carol. "Water Works." *Science and Children* 25 (April 1988): 15–17.

Vitale, John C. "How To Keep Your Students from Yawning at Art Museums." *Design* (U.S.) 79 (Fall 1977): 10–11.

Voris, Helen H., Maija Sedzielarz, and Carolyn P. Blackmon. *Teach the Mind, Touch the Spirit: A Guide to Focused Field Trips.* Chicago: Department of Education, Field Museum of Natural History, 1986.

Webster, Harriet. *Going Places: The Young Traveler's Guide and Activity Book.* New York: Charles Scribner's Sons, 1991.

Weinstein, Grace W. "Schools Where Education Comes Alive." *Parents* (June 1971): 33–37.

Wesley, John. *Pioneers.* Lakeside, CA: Interact, 1974.

What Works: Research about Teaching and Learning. Washington, DC: U.S. Department of Education, 1986.

Wheeler, James O. "Creating Local Field Trips: Seeing Geographical Principles through Empirical Eyes." *Journal of Geography,* Vol. 84, no. 5 (Sept.–Oct. 1985): 217–219.

Wiener, Harvey S. *Any Child Can Write: An At-Home Guide to Enhancing Your Child's Elementary Education.* Rev. ed. New York: Bantam Books, 1990.

Wildsmith, Brian. *Fishes.* New York: Oxford, 1968.

Williams, Frank E. *Classroom Ideas for Encouraging Thinking and Feeling.* National Schools Project.

Williams, Vera B. *Stringbean's Trip to the Shining Sea.* New York: Greenwillow, 1988.

———. *Three Days on a River in a Red Canoe.* New York: Greenwillow, 1981.

Wilson, James L. "Looking Around at the Zoo." *Science and Children* 21 (February 1984): 24–27.

Wood, Jacalyn K. "Take a Field Trip Close to Home." *Science and Children* 24 (October 1986): 26–27.

Workman, Brooke. "The Field Trip Course: 'Try It, You'll Like It'." *Clearing House* 49 (February 1976): 283–285.

Yenawine, Philip. *Colors.* New York: Museum of Modern Art in cooperation with Delacorte Press, 1991.

———. *Lines.* New York: Museum of Modern Art in cooperation with Delacorte Press, 1991.

———. *Shapes.* New York: Museum of Modern Art in cooperation with Delacorte Press, 1991.

————. *Stories.* New York: Museum of Modern Art in cooperation with Delacorte Press, 1991.

Zielinski, Edward J. "So You Want To Take a Field Trip." 1987. ED 299 079.

Zietlin, Patty. *Spin, Spider, Spin: Songs for a Greater Appreciation of Nature.* Baldwin, NY: Educational Activities, 1974.

Zoo: A Simulation of Caring for Animals in a Modern Zoo. Lakeside, CA: Interact. Three-ring notebook, 174 pages. (For more information write to Interact, Box 997, Lakeside, CA 92040.)

Index

128 • Index